I0176424

THE ILLUSION OF PEACE IN SOCIAL HIERARCHY

Is World Peace Achievable?

FRANCIS JEREMIAH SHARON

Contents

INTRODUCTION

When Herbert Marshall McLuhan In 1964 predicted that the world was becoming a global village, it was not an exaggerated statement. 50 years down the line, all parts of the world are being connected together by the internet, and other electronic communication media. Ideas and beliefs are also being shared at a rapid pace, although some beliefs and ideologies are being rejected (Nazism), some are being embraced globally (Democracy).

The advent of social media in the 21st century has procreated the spread of beliefs, and ideas through free speech, but it has also fostered cyber bullying and hate speech. There is also a popular whim of 'world peace' going around in the international community, and in all public discord. They are also organisations in place to achieve 'world peace', like the United Nations and the United Nations Security Council to name a few.

The delirium of 'world peace' is not going anytime soon, it is here to stay. Dissidents against the status quo are dealt with, either with soft or hard power. There is a growing illusion of achieving 'world peace', and adherents of this movement are suggesting ways of achieving this feat– non-violent resistance, pacifism, demonstrations, boycotts, ethical consumerism, and supporting anti-war candidates are some of the ploy they use to achieve their goals.

According to the Guinness Book of World Records, the largest anti-war rally recorded in human history took place in Rome (2004), with around three million people. Why? Because the United States was clamping down on terrorism, and protecting her security interests.

I do not believe in 'world peace', I believe 'world peace' is an illusion. The truth is we are always at aversion with people who are of different opinions, people we do not like, enmity with nature, enmity with animals, religious zealots are at enmity with spiritual forces, even Mother Nature is trying to kill you. Throughout the course of human history, man has maintained peace with his neighbours, but man has never achieved peace. Our successes in maintaining peace in certain situations, has led to boastful delusion and exaggerated beliefs of attaining 'world peace'.

The United States, which is a superpower of our time, is not at peace with herself. They are ideological battles between the far Right and Left, which I believe dialogue, can straighten out. What is a woman? Depends on who you ask.

This book does not view peace as the absence of armed conflict within a particular period, but rather peace as the lack of animosity, hatred, malice between individuals and countries at large. In this book let us view peace as 'heaven', I don't think angelic beings keep malice, or act hostile towards each other, do they? Let us surrogate that situation in Human/International relations, and debate if that is ever achievable.

Can we proceed?

THE CONCEPT OF PEACE IN INTERNATIONAL RELATIONS

"The peace of the world is disturbed by the military invasion of the Russian Federation on Ukraine. Europe is moved as the spectre of war rises again. Again war violence devastates human lives," – Alberto Fernandez speech in the opening of the 140th ordinary legislative session of Argentina's National Congress.

International relation is a subject everyone claims to be cognoscente in when a war breaks out, or hostility is impending. The breakout of the Russo-Ukrainian war in the first quarter of 2022, showed how *au fait* the general public was, when it came to understanding international relations. The media aired sentimental headlines supporting the Ukrainians, whilst condemning Russia for raging war and disturbing the 'World peace'.

In reality, the international community has never been at peace. Before the 'media outbreak' of the Russo-Ukrainian war in 2022, the war has actually been on-going since 2014. Which 'World Peace' was the Argentine president talking about? The general public are also quick to blame the 'Bigger guy' in a conflict, like the Israeli-Palestinian conflict and the Russo-Ukrainian war, claiming that they ought to 'know better'.

This chapter would expound on on-going wars, insurgency, and communal clashes plaguing the international community (as of time written), and how media bias, or should i say 'media cover-ups' by their respective governments, gives the average Gen Z the illusion that we are living in a 'peaceful era'.

War on terror

The Global War on Terrorism (GWOT) is an on-going international military campaign launched by the United States government following the September 11 attacks. The targets of the campaign are primarily Islamist groups located throughout the world, with the most prominent groups being al-Qaeda, as well as the Islamic State and their various franchise groups.

According to a 2021 study conducted by the Watson Institute for International and Public Affairs, the several post 9/11 wars participated in, by the United States, in her war against terror have caused the displacement, conservatively calculated, of 38 million people in Afghanistan, Pakistan, Iraq, Libya, Syria, Yemen, Somalia, and the Philippines. The study estimated these wars caused the deaths of 897,000 to 929,000 people, including over 364,000 civilians, and property damage cost $8 trillion. Where is the peace?

War of Dafur

The War in Darfur is a major armed conflict in the Darfur region of Sudan that began in February 2003 when the Sudan Liberation Movement (SLM) and the Justice and Equality Movement (JEM) rebel groups began fighting against the government of Sudan, which they accused of oppressing Darfur's non-Arab population. The government responded to attacks by carrying out a campaign of ethnic cleansing against Darfur's non-Arabs. This resulted in the death of hundreds of thousands of civilians and the indictment of Sudan's president, Omar al-Bashir, for genocide, war crimes, and crimes against humanity by the International Criminal Court.

In January 2010, the Centre for Research on the Epidemiology of Disasters published an article in a special issue of The Lancet. The article, entitled "Patterns of mortality rates in Darfur conflict", estimated with 95% confidence that the excess number of deaths during the war is between 178,258 and 461,520, with 80% of these due to disease. Where is the peace?

Kivu conflict

The Kivu conflict is an armed conflict in eastern Congo between the military of the Democratic Republic of the Congo (FARDC) and the Hutu Power group Democratic Forces for the Liberation of Rwanda (FDLR) that began in 2004. It has broadly consisted of three phases, the third of which is an on-going conflict. Prior to March 2009, the main combatant group against the FARDC was the National Congress for the Defence of the People (CNDP). Following the cessation of hostilities between these two forces, rebel Tutsi forces, formerly under the command of Laurent Nkunda, became the dominant opposition to the government forces.

According to CNDP, the conflict has left more than 1.4 million persons internally displaced, and has caused hundreds of thousands of excess deaths. Where is the peace?

Mexican drug War

The Mexican drug war is an on-going conflict between the Mexican government and various drug trafficking syndicates. When the Mexican military began to intervene in 2006, the government's main objective was to reduce drug-related violence. The Mexican government has asserted that their primary focus is dismantling the cartels, and preventing drug trafficking demand along with United States functionaries. Therefore, the conflict has been described as the Mexican theatre of the global war on drugs, as led by the United States federal government.

The official death toll of the Mexican drug war is at least 60,000. Estimates set the death toll above 120,000 killed by 2013, not including 27,000 missing. Where is the peace?

Syrian civil war

The Syrian civil war is an on-going multi-sided civil war in Syria fought between the Syrian Arab Republic led by Syrian president Bashar al-Assad and various domestic and foreign forces that oppose both the Syrian government and each other, in varying combinations.

Estimates of the total number of deaths in the Syrian Civil War, by opposition activist groups, vary between 499,657 and about 610,000. On 23 April 2016, the United Nations and Arab League Envoy to Syria put out an estimate of 400,000 that had died in the war. Where is the peace?

Rojava Islamist conflict

The Rojava-Islamist conflict is an on-going conflict and a major theater in the Syrian civil war, it started after fighting erupted between the Kurdish People's Protection Units (YPG) and Islamist rebel factions in the city of Ras al-Ayn. Kurdish forces launched a campaign in an attempt to take control of the Islamist-controlled areas in the governorate of al-Hasakah, and some parts of Raqqa and Aleppo governorates, after al-Qaeda in Syria used those areas to attack the YPG. The Kurdish groups and their allies' goal were also to capture Kurdish areas from the Arab Islamist rebels and strengthen the autonomy of the region of Rojava. The Syrian Democratic Forces would go on to take substantial territory from Islamist groups, in particular the Islamic State of Iraq and the Levant, provoking Turkish involvement in the Syrian Civil War.

According to YPG/SDF, 25,336 persons have been killed in the war, with about 100,000 Syrian Kurds fleeing to Turkey. Where is the peace?

Yemeni civil war

The Yemeni Civil War is an on-going multilateral civil war that began in late 2014 mainly between the Abdrabbuh Mansur Hadi-led Yemeni government and the Houthi armed movement, along with their supporters and allies. Both claim to constitute the official government of Yemen.

According to a United Nations estimate, by the end of 2021 the conflict in Yemen would have caused over 377,000 deaths, with 60% of them the result of hunger, lack of healthcare and unsafe water. The estimate also claims more than 10,200 children are known to have been killed or wounded as a direct result of the fighting. Where is the peace?

Tigray war

The Tigray War is an on-going civil war that began on 3rd November 2020 in the Tigray Region of Ethiopia. The local Tigray Defense Forces (TDF) are fighting the Ethiopian National Defense Force (ENDF), the Ethiopian Federal Police, regional police, and gendarmerie forces of the neighbouring Amhara and Afar regions with the involvement of the Eritrean Defence Forces (EDF). All sides, particularly the ENDF, EDF, and TDF have committed war crimes during the conflict.

Estimates claim that the Tigray war has seen up to half a million dead from violence and starvation. Where is the peace?

Russo-Ukrainian war

The Russo-Ukrainian War is an on-going war between Russia (together with pro-Russian separatist forces) and Ukraine. It began in February 2014 following the Ukrainian Revolution of Dignity, and initially focused on the status of Crimea and the Donbas, internationally recognised as part of Ukraine.

According to Reuters, at least 46,000 persons have been killed and 14 million persons displaced within Ukraine. The war has also created approximately $600 billion in Property damage. Where is the peace?

Internal conflict in Myanmar

Insurgencies have been on-going in Myanmar since 1948, the year the country, then known as Burma, gained independence from the United Kingdom. The conflict has largely been ethnic-based, with several ethnic armed groups fighting Myanmar's armed forces, the Tatmadaw, for self-determination. Despite numerous ceasefires and the creation of autonomous self-administered zones in 2008, many armed groups continue to call for independence, increased autonomy, or the federalisation of the country. The conflict is the world's longest on-going civil war, having spanned more than seven decades.

According to Reports, over 150,000 persons have been killed and 600,000–1,000,000 persons are internally displaced. Where is the peace?

Somali civil war

The Somali Civil War is an on-going civil war taking place in Somalia. It grew out of resistance to the military junta which was led by Siad Barre during the 1980s. From

1988 to 1990, the Somali Armed Forces began engaging in combat against various armed rebel groups, including the Somali Salvation Democratic Front in the northeast, the Somali National Movement in the northwest, and the United Somali Congress in the south. The clan-based armed opposition groups overthrew the Barre government in 1991.

According to Necrometrics, around 500,000 people are estimated to have been killed in Somalia since the start of the civil war in 1991. Where is the peace?

Ethnic conflict in South Sudan

Ethnic violence in South Sudan is an on-going conflict among varied ethnic groups in the country. South Sudan has 64 tribes with the largest being the Dinkas, who constitute about 35% of the population and predominate the government. The second largest are the Nuers. Conflict is often aggravated among nomadic groups over the issue of cattle and grazing land and is part of the wider Sudanese nomadic conflicts.

About 400,000 people were estimated to have been killed in the war by April 2018, including notable atrocities such as the 2014 Bentiu massacre. Where is the peace?

Iraqi Conflict

The Iraqi conflict is an on-going armed conflict that began with the 2003 invasion of Iraq by a United States-led coalition that toppled the government of Saddam Hussein. The conflict continued as an insurgency, emerged to oppose the occupying forces and the post-invasion Iraqi government. The United States officially withdrew from the country in 2011, but became involved in 2014 at the head of a new coalition. The main phase of the conflict ended following the defeat of the Islamic State of Iraq and the Levant (ISIL) in the country in 2017, but a low-level ISIL insurgency is on-going in the rural north parts of the country.

Population-based studies produce estimates of the number of Iraq war casualties ranging from 151,000 violent deaths as of June 2006 (per the Iraq Family Health Survey) to 1,033,000 excess deaths (per the 2007 Opinion Research Business survey). All estimates of Iraq war casualties are disputed. Where is the peace?

Colombian conflict

The Colombian conflict is an on-going conflict which began in 1964, and is a war between the government of Colombia, far-right paramilitary groups, crime syndicates, and far-left guerrilla groups such as the Revolutionary Armed Forces of Colombia (FARC), the National Liberation Army (ELN) and the Popular Liberation Army (EPL), fighting each other to increase their influence in Colombian territory.

According to a study by Colombia's National Centre for Historical Memory, 220,000 people have died in the conflict between 1958 and 2013, most of them civilians, and more than five million civilians were forced from their homes between 1985 and 2012, generating the world's second largest population of internally displaced persons (IDPs). Where is the peace?

Insurgency in the Maghreb

The insurgency in the Maghreb is an on-going Islamist insurgency in the Maghreb and Sahel regions of North

Africa that followed on from the end of the Algerian Civil War in 2002. The Algerian militant group, Salafist Group for Preaching and Combat (GSPC) allied itself with al-Qaeda to eventually become al-Qaeda in the Islamic Maghreb (AQIM). The Algerian and other Maghreb governments fighting the militants have worked with the United States and the United Kingdom since 2007.

The on-going conflict with the GSPC has resulted to a significant number of casualties in Algeria, with over 1,100 killed in clashes with Islamist rebels in 2002. In 2003, a total 1,162 were killed in clashes in Algeria, followed by 429 killed in 2004, 488 killed in 2005, and 323 killed in 2006. Where is the peace?

Mali war

The Mali War is an on-going armed conflict that started in January 2012 between the northern and southern parts of Mali in Africa. On 16 January 2012, several insurgent groups began fighting a campaign against the Malian government for independence or greater autonomy for northern Mali, which they called Azawad. The National Movement for the Liberation of Azawad (MNLA), an organization fighting to make this area of Mali an independent homeland for the Tuareg people, had taken control of the region by April 2012.

According to estimates 1,200–1,500 persons have been killed or captured, including 859 ISGS (Islamic State in the Greater Sahara) members killed and 169 others captured during Operation Barkhane between January 2020 and April 2021. Where is the peace?

Nigeria bandit conflict

The bandit conflict in northwest Nigeria is an on-going conflict between the country's government and various gangs and ethnic militias. Starting in 2011, the insecurity remaining from the conflict between the Fulani and Hausa ethnic groups quickly allowed other criminal and jihadist elements to form in the region.

Data from the Armed Conflict Location & Event Data Project shows that bandits were responsible for more than 2,600 civilian deaths in 2021 – many more than those attributed to rebel groups Boko Haram and the Islamic State West Africa Province in the same year – and almost three times the number of victims in 2020. Where is the peace?

Allied Democratic forces insurgency

The Allied Democratic Forces insurgency is an on-going conflict waged by the Allied Democratic Forces in Uganda and the Democratic Republic of the Congo, against the governments of those two countries and the United Nations Organization Stability Mission in the Democratic Republic of the Congo (MONUSCO). The insurgency began in 1996, intensifying in 2013, resulting in hundreds of deaths.

According to reports, 3,424 persons have been killed and 150,000+ persons displaced. Where is the peace?

Insurgency in Cabo Delgado

The insurgency in Cabo Delgado is an ongoing Islamist insurgency in the region of East Africa and the Cabo Delgado Province, Mozambique, mainly fought between militant Islamists and jihadists attempting to establish an

Islamic state in the region. Civilians have been the main targets of terrorist attacks by Islamist militants.

According to reports the conflict has left nearly 4,000 people dead and displaced 800,000, which is half the province's population. Where is the peace?

Moro conflict

The Moro conflict is an insurgency in the Mindanao region of the Philippines, which has involved multiple armed groups, and has been on-going since March 1968.

Casualty statistics vary for the conflict, though the conservative estimates of the Uppsala Conflict Data Program indicate that at least 6,015 people were killed in armed conflict between the government of the Philippines and the Abu Sayyaf (ASG), Bangsamoro Islamic Freedom Fighters (BIFF), Moro Islamic Liberation Front (MILF), and Moro National Liberation Front (MNLF) factions between 1989 and 2012. Where is the peace?

Papua conflict

The Papua conflict is an on-going conflict in Western New Guinea between Indonesia and the Free Papua Movement. Subsequent to the withdrawal of the Dutch administration from the Netherlands New Guinea in 1962 and implementation of Indonesian administration in 1963, the Free Papua Movement has conducted a low-intensity guerrilla war against Indonesia through the targeting of its military, police, and civilian populations.

Observers of the conflict estimate that between 100,000 and 500,000 West Papuans have been killed since the Indonesian takeover of West Papua in the 1960s. Where is the peace?

Kurdish–Turkish conflict

The Kurdish–Turkish conflict is an on-going armed conflict between the Republic of Turkey and various Kurdish insurgent groups who have either demanded separation from Turkey to create an independent Kurdistan, or attempted to secure autonomy and greater political and cultural rights for Kurds inside the Republic of Turkey.

Since the conflict began, more than 40,000 have died, with majority of the casualties being Kurdish civilians. Both sides were accused of numerous human rights abuses during the conflict. The European Court of Human Rights has condemned Turkey for thousands of human rights abuses. Where is the peace?

Insurgency in Khyber Pakhtunkhwa

The insurgency in Khyber Pakhtunkhwa, is an on-going armed conflict involving Pakistan, and Islamist militant groups such as the Tehrik-i-Taliban Pakistan (TTP), Jundallah, Lashkar-e-Islam (LeI), TNSM, al-Qaeda, and their Central Asian allies such as the ISIL–Khorasan (ISIL), Islamic Movement of Uzbekistan, East Turkistan Movement, Emirate of Caucasus, and elements of organized crime. Formerly a war, it is now a low-level insurgency.

According to reports, over 6 million civilians have been displaced during the conflict. Where is the peace?

Philippines drug war

The Philippine drug war is an on-going anti-drug policy and actions of the Philippine government under President Rodrigo Duterte. According to former Philippine National

16

Police Chief and Senator Ronald dela Rosa, the policy is aimed at "the neutralization of illegal drug personalities nationwide."

Estimates of the death toll vary. Officially, 6,229 drug personalities have been killed as of March 2022. News organizations and human rights groups claim the death toll is over 12,000. The victims included 54 children in the first year. Opposition senators claimed in 2018 that over 20,000 have been killed. Where is the peace?

Libyan crisis

The Libyan Crisis is an on-going humanitarian crisis and political-military instability occurring in Libya, beginning with the Arab Spring protests of 2011, which led to a civil war, foreign military intervention, and the ousting and death of Muammar Gaddafi. The civil war's aftermath and proliferation of armed groups led to violence and instability across the country, which erupted into renewed civil war in 2014.

Estimates of deaths in the Libyan Civil War vary with figures from 2,500 to 25,000 given between March 2 and October 2, 2011. An exact figure is hard to ascertain, partly due to a media clamp-down by the Libyan government. Where is the peace?

Sudan's conflict in South Kordofan and Blue Nile

The Sudanese conflict in South Kordofan and Blue Nile is an ongoing armed conflict in the Sudanese southern states of South Kordofan and Blue Nile between the Sudanese Army (SAF) and Sudan People's Liberation Movement-North (SPLM-N), a northern affiliate of the Sudan People's Liberation Movement (SPLM) in South Sudan.

According to SAF there have been 109,300 Casualties and losses in the conflict in South Kordofan and Blue Nile. Where is the peace?

Anglophone crisis

The Anglophone Crisis is an on-going civil war in the Southern Cameroons regions of Cameroon, part of the long-standing Anglophone problem. Following the suppression of Cameroonian protests, Ambazonian separatists in the Anglophone territories of Northwest Region and Southwest Region (collectively known as Southern Cameroons) launched a guerrilla campaign against Cameroonian security forces, and later unilaterally proclaimed the restoration of independence. In November 2017, the government of Cameroon declared war on the separatists and sent its army into the Anglophone regions.

According to reports 4,000 civilians have been killed and 700,000 internally displaced, resulting in 63,800 refugees in Nigeria. Where is the peace?

Lord resistance Army Insurgency

The Lord's Resistance Army insurgency is an on-going guerrilla campaign waged by the Lord's Resistance Army (LRA) insurgent group since 1987. The movement is led by Joseph Kony, who proclaims himself the "spokesperson" of God and a spirit medium. It aims to overthrow Yoweri Museveni's Ugandan government and establish a theocratic state based on a version of the Ten Commandments and Acholi tradition.

During the insurgency 1.5 million civilians have been displaced and an estimated 100,000 civilians killed. Where is the peace?

Nagorno-Karabakh conflict

The Nagorno-Karabakh conflict is an on-going ethnic and territorial conflict between Armenia and Azerbaijan over the disputed region of Nagorno-Karabakh. The conflict has its origins in the early 20th century, but the present conflict began in 1988, when the Karabakh Armenians demanded transferring Karabakh from Soviet Azerbaijan to Soviet Armenia. The conflict escalated into a full-scale war in the early 1990s which later transformed into a low-intensity conflict until four-day escalation in April 2016 and then into another full-scale war in 2020.

According to official figures released by the belligerents, Armenia and Artsakh lost 3,825 troops, with 187 servicemen missing in action, while Azerbaijan claimed 2,906 of their troops were killed, with 6 missing in action. Where is the peace?

Cabinda war

The Cabinda War is an on-going separatist insurgency, waged by the Front for the Liberation of the Enclave of Cabinda (FLEC) against the government of Angola. FLEC aims at the restoration of the self-proclaimed Republic of Cabinda, located within the borders of the Cabinda province of Angola.

The Cabinda war has left approximately 30,000 persons killed leaving 25,000 displaced. Where is the peace?

Other unrest, insurgency and armed conflict around the world include: Terrorism in Egypt, Katanga Insurgency (Democratic Republic of the Congo), Chiapas conflict (Mexico), Islamic state Insurgency in Tunisia, Insurgency in Paraguay, BLM protests (United States), Biafran Unrest (Nigeria). Are we really at peace?

A friend of mine once uttered a renowned statement hazardously used by conformist and the general populace today:

"We are living in the most peaceful era in human history"

The illusion!

To prove that assumption wrong, researchers at the University of Colorado in Boulder plotted data from the Correlates of War Project's data set, one widely used in political science, to find out whether we are really in the midst of a period of true harmony. The database includes the year of onset and number of battle deaths for 95 interstate conflicts between 1823 and 2003. The Crimean War, for example, kicked off in 1853 and eventually killed about 264,000 soldiers in battle. World War II killed more than 16.6 million. And the Yom Kippur War killed some 14,400 soldiers in 1973. Data on civil wars and non-state actors, such as terrorist groups, were not included in this analysis.

Computer scientist Aaron Clauset, who was in charge of the research, crunched the data as if they represented any other statistical relationship, looking for trends and calculating the normal range of fluctuation in both battle deaths and years between conflicts. Numbers of battle dead for a given war ranged from 1000—the minimum number in the data set—to the millions killed in World War II. For the purposes of the study, Clauset defined a large war as one whose battle death toll falls within the upper quartile of total battle deaths over the past 2 centuries. Basically, that means anything with more than 26,625 deaths.

Then he developed a series of computer models to replay the period from 1823 to 2003, using only statistical likelihood from the data to determine the frequency and severity of imaginary interstate wars. For one thing, Clauset found the unimaginable carnage of World War II was not, in fact, a statistical anomaly; its death toll falls well within the expected range for war deaths.

But he also found that, statistically speaking, going several decades without a large war simply is not a rare event—and that peace can quickly be upended by another large conflict. From a statistical perspective, there's nothing special about the current 'long peace'. In order for our present peaceful era to become meaningfully aberrant—that is, for it to represent a real change in our ability to get along—it would have to last for another 100 to 140 years.

Clauset claims that the statistical risk of another large scale war sometime soon is not small, although the number of unknowable variables about the future makes it difficult to forecast with any confidence.

Where is the peace?

THE CONCEPT OF PEACE WITHIN PEER GROUPS

There is no peace between friends or peers. I believe what exist between friends are mutual respect and expectations. In human psychology having friends is necessary for survival, friends and alliances have shaped human civilization, but contrary to popular beliefs propagated by the media; i believe you are not at peace with your friends.

Conformity

According to Kulsum and Jauhar, Conformity is an influence which stems from social environment, in which individuals change their attitudes, and behaviors in accordance with existing social norms. According to John W. Santrock, Peer group is a group of friends, who have close and mutual relationships. Next according to Santrock, Conformity is something a person does when he is in a group. Thus, conformity occurs because of a strong desire to maintain peace, gain emotional support and desire to be accepted in a group.

Psychologist Noam Shpancer explains on his blog, *"We are often not even aware when we are conforming. It is our home base, our default mode."* Shpancer says you conform because social acceptance is built into your brain. To thrive, you know you need friends because outcasts are cut off from valuable resources. Conformity is a survival mechanism.

In that way peace in peer groups is maintained through conformity, once a member refuses to conform to the ethics of a group, peace breaks down and strive reigns. I believe before Martin Luther went against the popular canon of the Catholic Church and promulgated the protestant reformation, peace was maintained in the catholic realm by conformity. I believe a lot of people chose to conform to the catholic doctrine rather than being tried for heresy. Where is the peace?

Friendship is symbiotic

Reiterating on what I stated before, 'what exist between friends are mutual respect and expectations'. Elucidating on 'expectations', I opine that friendship is symbiotic. Friendship exists in mutual co-operation for the benefit of each individual bounded in that relationship.

Friendship might have varying definition according to how best it fits you, but symbiosis has no varying definition. Symbiosis describes close interactions between two or more different species. It is different from regular interactions between species because, in a symbiotic relationship, the two species in the relationship live together. Many organisms in nature are involved in symbiotic relationships because this interaction provides benefits to both species.

Friendship is a symbiotic relationship that exists among members of the same specie (human to human). No friendship is selfless. All friendships are for mutual benefits. When two or more people discover each other, and fulfil each other's respective needs, a relationship forms, friendship or equivalent.

Think of it this way, you help a friend because he had helped you in your hard times. That help might be something tangible or intangible. Sometimes you help a person because you know he might be of help to you in future. Sometimes you help someone because you feel they are in dire need of it. When we make friends we create expectations from them, that is why betrayal is a common anecdote between friends. What constitutes the betrayal? Fallen expectations.

You can call that relationship whatever you want – symbiotic, healthy, unhealthy, toxic, etc. But it is all based on the fulfilment of needs.

In that way, peace in "friendship" is maintained through symbiosis. What happens when a symbiotic relationship breaks down, what happens when one person gives too much in a relationship? What happens when ones needs and boundaries are not respected in a relationship? I guess the peace breaks down. Truth is that, it was never there. Where is the peace?

Labelling theory

Friends are labels we give to each other. Labels leads to segregation, segregation leads to pique, pique results to hate. Where's the peace?

When you think of friends, you think of cliques or squads. If you don't belong to a group, you feel left out or unwanted. We create these groups to feel like we belong, but by doing so we make others feel left out, It is ironic. Having a 'best friend' sends out the message to everyone else, that they are inferior to the person you have chosen as a best friend. Putting cliques and best friends aside, when you call a person your 'friend', you are inadvertently calling everyone else around you a stranger, enemy, or an outsider. Where is the peace?

"I am convinced that men hate each other because they fear each other. They fear each other because they don't know each other, and they don't know each other because they don't communicate with each other, and they don't communicate with each other because they are separated from each other" – Martin Luther King, Jr.

According to Martin Luther king Jr., hate breeds when people are isolated or separated from each other, he opines that hate stems from lack of communication which stems from separation. These days Labels separates people. In High school, you can have a clique of friends who are also isolated from other clique of friends. Most times these different cliques are like the political far left and far right, always at enmity with each other. I believe that nearly 90% of peer groups are at ends with some other peer group, and relatively that's how gang rivalries are formed. Where's the peace?

On July 6, 2012, Skylar Neese a 16 year old girl living in Morgantown, West Virginia was brutally stabbed and killed by her two best friends, Shelia Eddy and Rachel Shoaf. When authorities asked Rachel Shoaf during her confession, why they killed Skylar Neese, she simply replied, "We didn't like her." Where is the peace?

Friendship is an illusion. No one is your friend unconditionally. Relationships are symbiotic, that is how peace is maintained. Most times in an attempt to make 'friends' we lose ourselves and claim to be someone who we are not. In an attempt to maintain peace with our peers, we give into pressures and conform. Conformity is an attempt of maintaining peace.

Here's a research which supports my thesis that friendship is an illusion. The research shows that we may have only half as many friends as we believe.

Alex Pentland a Massachusetts Institute of Technology researcher asked students on a business management course to rank how close they were to each of their classmates, on a scale of 0 to 5. Zero meant 'I do not know this person', 1 was defined as 'I recognise this person but we never talked' while an acquaintance merited a score of 2. Only scale 3 and above denoted friendship. A 3 described a friend, 4 were reserved for close friends and to get a 5 someone had to be a best friend.

Importantly, the 84 men and women aged 23 to 38 were asked to predict how the other person would score them. Analysis of the results showed that 94 per cent of the students expected their feelings of friendship to be reciprocated. But that happened in only 53 per cent of cases. In summary the research shows that most people we consider our friends may be less keen on us than we are on them.

Other research has found that as few as a third of 'friendships' are mutual. One explanation is that we simply assume our feelings are shared –because the thought that the people we value do not feel the same way about us, would be too hurtful. It is also possible that many unreciprocated friendships are aspirational, with people naming popular or powerful types as friends, even when they do not know them very well. The rise of social media means the definition of friendship has become blurred.

Another study has shown that four in ten people have a 'friend' they regularly see who they actually cannot stand. The research, polled 2000 Brits and found most have an average of 16 friends – including three they do not get on with. The study found that a quarter of people have told this person that they do not like them, and half have tried to 'phase them out' after a fight.

They found that the most common reasons for disliking your mates included having nothing in common, being too bossy, having different opinions or acting differently while drunk. People end up socialising with someone they would not usually choose as a friend, perhaps through work, friends-of-friends or through your partner.

INTRAPERSONAL
PEACE

"Your sense of self is just that—a sense. The person you imagine yourself to be is a story you tell to yourself and to others differently depending on the situation and the story changes over time." – an excerpt from David McCreary book "You are not so smart why you have too many friends on Facebook, why your memory is mostly fiction, and 46 other ways you're deluding yourself"

Y ou are not at peace with yourself! A lot of people might not be aware of this, but they are multiple "YOUS" and every one of you is at conflict with you (whichever one it is). But firstly what is intrapersonal peace? Does it exist?

Intrapersonal peace simply translates to peace within oneself. But how can one achieve peace within oneself if one encompasses multiple selves. The concept of multiple selves is one that is not widely accepted in human psychology, but they are a lot of evidence to the contrary. The self is not the physical body. If so, my 'self' would still be there if I got shot and died. But most people would say that a dead body does not contain the self; the self, resides in the dimension of the mental and cultural and is not really reducible to the physical and biological.

Most personality psychology research relies on the notion that humans have a single self that is the result of the individual's thoughts, feelings, and behaviours that can be described. This idea has been challenged by many theorists over the last 60 years. Carl Gustav Jung was the first to describe systematically the origin of the selves, which can arise from personal experiences or can develop from stereotyped roles, such as the role of a teacher or a famous person. Selves can become the 'persona' or the 'shadow' or can be present in the form of an 'archetype,' which altogether construct the personality.

Andras Angyal postulated that the mind is made up of subsystems that interact with one another and can result in mental pressure, intrusion or invasion in the case of conflicting interests. Alright, to put this notion to test, I will ask a question which would put your multiple selves to trance.

Daniel Kahneman Theory of Multiple selves

Imagine you are preparing to go on a two-week vacation, and at the end of this vacation, you will drink a potion that will erase all the memories from those two weeks. What would your decision be, and what will you spend your time doing, during those two weeks?

That weird feeling you are having thinking about this is the conflict between your experiencing and remembering self. The paradox between the experiencing self and remembering self is one postulated by Daniel Kahneman, a Nobel prize winner and pioneering researcher within behavioural economics (This is one of the many theories of selves).

Daniel Kahneman describes the experiencing self as an example of the fast, intuitive, unconscious mode of thinking that operates in the present moment, focusing on the quality of our experience in our life. Each moment of the experiencing self lasts about 3 seconds, most of them vanishing without a trace. It drags your current self around in pursuit of new memories, anticipating them based on old memories. The current self is happy when experiencing things. It likes to be in the flow.

The remembering self is an example of the slow, rational, conscious mode of thinking that tells the story of our experience, how we think about our experience. It is the remembering self that has made all the big decisions. It is happy when you can sit back and reflect on your life up to this point and feel content. It is happy when you tell people stories about the things you have seen and done.

Kahneman suggests that the self in charge of making decisions in your life is usually the remembering one. But the question I asked earlier goes against the norm, if there is nothing to remember, what will you do? Well that is a mental conflict on its own. Where is the peace?

Why do people have a hard time in quitting their addictions? Well, I believe it is the conflict between the experiencing self and remembering self at play here. Yes, you agreed to quit drinking, but you see yourself going back to drinking, for the fun, for the thrill, that is your experiencing self-winning here. Remembering the event, you feel gross and betrayed, that is your remembering self. That short moment you talk to yourself before picking up the beer is paradigm of conflict between yourselves. To maintain peace oneself must lose, you capitulate. You drink!

Why can you not approach your crush in class? Well if you are someone with anxiety issues, or you have been rejected before, it is the experiencing self and remembering self at war here. Your remembering self does not want a bad memory of rejection again; it plays previous events of rejection and tells you, 'you are not good enough'. To maintain peace oneself must lose, you capitulate. You do not approach her!

Or did you eventually approach her, congratulations! Your experiencing self-won. We are subconsciously having these battles of selves within ourselves, but we do not pay attention, because we think 'we are probably one person'. Combating addiction is a conflict of the selves;

fear is a conflict of the selves. In fact, we can feel a whole lot of conflict between ourselves, especially when it comes to making decisions, and decisions arise from situations. Thus 'ourselves' is largely a function of the situation.

They are many other concept of selves, I will illuminate on a few here.

Gregg Henriques Theory of Multiple Selves

Gregg Henriques, a professor of psychology at James Madison University, in his blog describes the human self as consisting of three related, but also separable domains. The first domain is the experiential self. The second portion of the human self is called the private self-consciousness system. The third portion of the self is the public self or persona.

The experiential self is the part of you that 'disappears' when you enter deep sleep, flickers on and off as you dream, and then comes back online as you wake up. The private self-consciousness system is the portion of your being that verbally narrates what is happening and why, this self tries to make sense of what is going on. As you read this book and think about what it means, this is your verbal narrator working. The persona self refers to the public image that you attempt to project to others, which in turn interacts with how other people actually see you.

Now how are these three selves postulated by Gregg at war with themselves? Have you ever dared yourself to stay awake throughout the night, but rather fell asleep? That is a war between your experiential self and your private self-consciousness. To maintain peace oneself must lose, you capitulate. You sleep! Sometimes unconsciously.

Where is the peace?

Brian Little Theory of Multiple Selves

Brian Little, a personality psychologist at Cambridge University, also has a trinity self-theory to propose. Little breaks down his theory into three broad strokes, each pertaining to a different 'layer' of what he suggests are most people's selves.

According to Little's theory, the first layer of you is 'biogenic.' In layperson's terms, this means that your first 'self' basically comes down to biology and what your genes tell you to do. Little describes the second layer of 'self' as 'sociogenic' — that is, how our surroundings, such as our family, neighbourhood, or culture, influence us. Little's final personality layer is the idiogenic self. This version of yourself is basically the one that you cultivate based on your interests, likes, dislikes, passions, and so on and forth.

How does Little's selves conflict each other? Ever thought of being born in the wrong body? Never? Well trans-genders do. I believe there is a conflict between their biogenic and sociogenic self. The Idiogenic and Sociogenic, conflict occurs every day among individuals. You want to be a Disc Jockey but your family wants you to be a doctor. You study medicine and go through life depressed, not finding home. Why? There are conflicts between selves going on. Who are you?

Where is the peace?

THE ZEITGEIST OF PEACE

"May there be peace in the heavens, peace in the atmosphere, peace on the earth. Let there be coolness in the water, healing in the herbs and peace radiating from the trees. Let there be harmony in the planets and in the stars, and perfection in eternal knowledge. May everything in the universe be at peace. Let peace pervade everywhere, at all times. May I experience that peace within my own heart."

— *Yajur Veda 36.17 Hinduism*

How did peace become the Zeitgeist of this era? Well I believe it stems from the trauma and pain inflicted by the wars that plagued Europe, and then the world from the 19th to 20th century.

The Crimean war in the 19th century exposed the brutality and atrocities of war to the average populace; it was the first war that received mass media coverage, and due to the mundane attitude of the war it had to be brought to a halt. Even Napoleon III also had a grotesque feeling after seeing the war casualties during the Franco-Prussian war. World War I would be more deadly to mankind. The allies who won the war, imposed hash sanctions on the axis especially Germany to maintain peace, well as we will discuss in subsequent chapters, peace not well maintained is dangerous. The Advent of Adolf Hitler and his monstrous atrocities towards the Jews would never be forgotten. Hitler's war would usher in the Pax Atomica, the illusion of peace we are experiencing now.

Going back in time peace was maintained through alliances between different nations, these alliances were codified through royal marriages. Two examples are Hermodike I in 800BC and Hermodike II in 600BC; they were Greek princesses from the house of Agamemnon who married kings from what is now Central Turkey. The union of Phrygia/Lydia with Aeolian Greeks resulted in regional peace, which facilitated the transfer of ground-breaking technological skills into Ancient Greece.

Apart from royal marriages, kingdoms have sometimes used ruthless measures to impose peace upon the vanquished, some of which includes the destruction of cultural heritages. An example of this was in 79AD, when the Romans destroyed the Jewish temple, exiled the Jews and renamed the area to Palestine (Formally called Judea and Samaria), a name that has stood till today.

From the early 20th century, philosophers and peace theorist have created organisation, awards and all sorts of dogma to promote and eventually achieve 'world peace' (some of which will be elucidated here),but they have all failed or deviated from their main goal, maybe because mankind is mischievous on her own.

The United Nations
The United Nations (UN) is an international organization whose stated aims are to facilitate cooperation in international law, international security, economic development, social progress, human rights, and achieving world peace. The United Nations was founded in 1945 after World War II to replace the League of Nations.

Historically, the United Nations has a good record of ignoring injustice and genocide going on around the world. In Bosnia, the United Nations promised to defend the Bosniaks in Srebrenica and Žepa, but then did nothing as they were massacred by the Serbs. In Rwanda, the United Nations stood by and watched, as the most horrendous genocide since the Holocaust took place, refusing to intervene.

In the Israeli-Palestinian Conflict, the United Nations has clearly shown tremendous bias against Israel. In 2018 alone, the United Nations condemned Israel 21 times,

Iran, North Korea, Syria, and Myanmar each once, and Hamas, Algeria, Sudan, Venezuela, Zimbabwe, Turkey, and Somalia not at all. For context, Myanmar is literally practicing ethnic cleansing, and the United Nations issued one condemnation against it. For all of the United Nation's history, 40% of its resolutions have been against Israel.

The United Nations is not just useless though, it is far worse. As long as the United Nations maintains its veneer of goodness, whatever it says and does is endowed with a halo. The United Nation's largest voting bloc– more than half of it, is made up of nondemocratic countries. They can pass whatever they agree on, and have it given a halo of goodness.

The Ukrainian President; Volodymyr Zelensky said something that was intellectually profound in his speech to the United Nations, when speaking on Russian atrocities in Ukraine.

Zelensky opined that the United Nations was an utter failure, and the organisation should dissolve itself, if it would not work to end Russia's war on his country. He was right. Long fetishized by progressives around the globe as the last bulwark of civilization against unending war, the United Nations has proven singularly inept at actually preventing violence and isolating dangerous regimes. In fact, it often empowers them.

Russia's presence as a permanent member at the Security Council's table — especially now, in the face of the sickening images of its war crimes in Ukraine — makes a mockery both of the United Nations as an organization and the principles it claims to stand for.

The same might be said of China's permanent membership. Beijing has been waging a brutal internal war against the Uyghurs for years, while facing no real repercussions from a global body ostensibly dedicated to securing all human rights, everywhere. It seems like the powerful countries that designed the United Nations structured it to be certain that they could always thwart any United Nations action to hold them accountable.

The United Nations has proofed herself to be utterly incapable of succeeding in its mission. Believers in its principles should be seeking something better to replace it. The UN's failure has been multifaceted and cannot be ascribed to one single cause. It is partly a failure of leadership, combined with poor management, discipline, and widespread inefficiency, as well as a deep-seated culture of corruption.

But we cannot take it all away from the United Nations. The United Nations has been successful in some areas that have to do with helping refuges, providing food and engaging in peace keeping missions. Almost all of these occur after the damage has been done on the war-torn populace, and after they have failed to protect the basic human rights of individuals that were lost during the wars, the United Nations then come in with their palliatives. Ridiculous!

Some of The United Nations Ludibrious accomplishments are:

1. The United Nations has sent over 69 peacekeeping missions to various regions, including Western Sahara, Central African Republic, Cyprus, Lebanon, India, Pakistan, etc. Currently, the United Nations deploys over 125,000 personnel.

2. The United Nations provided food to 97 million people in 80 countries, majorly in war zones.

3. UNICEF supplies vaccines to reach 45 per cent of the world's children under five with its partners.

4. More than 60 million refugees fleeing persecution, violence, and war have received aid from the Office of the United Nations High Commissioner for Refugees (UNHCR) since 1951. there are more than 42 million refugees, asylum-seekers, and internally displaced persons, mostly women, and children, who are receiving food, shelter, medical aid, education, and repatriation assistance from the United Nations.

5. The United Nations has raised awareness over multiple social issues, from the first United Nations conference on the environment (Stockholm, 1972), the first world conference on women (Mexico City, 1985), the first international conference on human rights (Teheran, 1968), the first world population conference (Bucharest, 1974) and the first world climate conference (Geneva, 1979.

6. The International Fund for Agricultural Development (IFAD) provides low-interest loans and grants to very poor rural people. Since 1978, IFAD has invested more than $15 billion, helping more than 430 million women and men to grow and sell more food, increase their incomes and provide for their families. Currently, IFAD supports more than 240 programs and projects in 147 countries.

The *League* of Nations

The principal forerunner of the United Nations was the League of Nations. It was created at the Paris Peace Conference of 1919, and emerged from the advocacy of United States president; Woodrow Wilson and other idealists during World War I. The Covenant of the League of Nations was included in the Treaty of Versailles in 1919, and the League was based in Geneva until its dissolution as a result of World War II and replaced by the United Nations.

The League of Nations had several integral weaknesses that finally led to its demise, some of which are:

- America's isolation: The American president Woodrow Wilson made the organization in order to prevent any future war in Europe. The United States Congress rejected the treaty and America was not able to be involved in it. It made the League of Nations quite paralyzed as the founding member was not involved and was not able to enforce the rules during crises.

- Decisions were slow and usually not obeyed: The League of Nations was an unwieldy organization as decisions in international crises were very slow, and when they made a decision, it was usually too late, and even if they were not, their decisions were not taken seriously, and this showed their ineffectiveness. The organization was also not able to take action against their members.

- The League of Nations was very ineffective at enforcing the policies, as it had no army. When the League of Nations enforced the Treaty of

Versailles, Adolph Hitler broke the treaty and ordered the Germans to re-militarize the Rhineland and Saarland. The League of Nations was not able to do a thing.

- League of Nations was ineffective as the leading members (Britain and France) were also using the organization to their own benefit. When the Italians were invading Abyssinia (modern day Ethiopia), the League of Nations condemned the actions of the Italian state, but was not able to take any action against it. Moreover, Britain and France ensured backdoor negotiations that said that they will pardon Italy if they support the Allies against Germany. (Promptly, the Italians betrayed it).

Peace theorist and philosophers also introduced peace prizes to promote, and encourage peace within individuals and countries at large, with the forerunner being the Nobel peace prize.

Nobel peace prize

The Nobel peace prize is awarded annually, to internationally notable persons following the prize's creation in the will of Alfred Nobel. According to Nobel's will, the Peace Prize shall be awarded to the person who *"shall have done the most or the best work for fraternity between nations, for the abolition or reduction of standing armies, and for the holding and promotion of peace congresses."*

Some of the laureate of the Nobel peace prize have been controversial, perhaps most notably, Abiy Ahmed, the prime minister of Ethiopia, who was awarded the prize in 2019 for helping to end his country's long-running war with Eritrea. The prize committee cited his *"efforts to achieve peace and international cooperation, and in particular for his decisive initiative to resolve the border conflict with neighbouring Eritrea."*

Abiy went on to conduct a brutal war in northern Ethiopia's Tigray region, in which both sides have been accused of a wide range of war crimes. Another controversial laureate is former United States President Barack Obama, who was nominated for the prize before he had been in office for a month and received the award before he had served even a year. Obama went on to increase United States troop levels in Afghanistan during part of his presidency, and he accelerated the use of drone strikes against individuals and groups seen as enemies of the United States.

Sweden, gifting the Nobel peace prize to underserving individuals, and the shady nomination process involved, shows that the prize is slowly losing it credibility, and when it loses credibility, it loses the potential impact the prize can have on world peace. Other charades known as peace prizes includes Student Peace Prize, Gandhi Peace Prize, and Sydney Peace Prize.

Over the eons different Ideologies and theories of Peace have been propagated and practised by individuals, and some members of the international community. The problem with these ideologies and theories is that none has best shown to achieve peace. I will elucidate on some of these ideologies in the subsequent pages.

Pacifism
Pacifism covers a spectrum of views ranging from the belief that international disputes can, and should all be resolved via peaceful behaviours; to calls for the abolition

of various organizations which tend to institutionalize aggressive behaviours, such as the military, or arms manufacturers; to opposition to any organization or society that might rely in any way upon governmental force. Absolute pacifism opposes violent behaviour under all circumstance, including defence of self and others.

The problem with pacifism is how does it deal with evil? The Nazis are murdering everyone who is not a physically perfect ethnic German and pacifism teaches you that fighting them is wrong? You idealize peaceful resistance though it does not matter if the enemy will just mow you down. Even Ghandi had a pacifist view, he begged the Jews to show no resistance so they would be on the more moral side, and more of them died.

The Soviet Union are murdering Christians, Muslims, and political rivals; they are blocking freedom of speech and the press, and starving millions of Ukrainians, a cold war that ensues in the following decades between the free west and the tyrannical Soviet Union is considered wrong by a pacifist, because they consider shows of force as a violent response to the soviet evil war machine.

The ISIS are imposing oppressive fundamentalist Sharia law, they are murdering Shia Muslims and Christians, and bringing back sex slave markets, and a pacifist thinks that it is evil to fight such a thing, so as to prevent it from metamorphosing into something more sinister. By refusing to defend freedom, they enable its destruction; they end up blaming the victims, whether it is the Islamic terrorists killing people to coerce the rest into submission to it heretical system, or Kurdish women living in fear in the ISIS controlled areas, so that they would not end up as sex slaves.

44

Your neighbour is beating his wife, and a pacifist thinks that it is wrong for her to fight back so that he does not kill her? A pacifist in that situation would not physically come to her defence because they think all violence is wrong.

In 1964, United States President, Ronald Rogan gave a speech which can be interpreted as a snare against Pacifism, in his speech he preached against accommodating the tyrannical Soviet Union. Some of the excerpt of his speech goes.

"...their (his political opponents) policy of accommodation is appeasement (pacifism); and it gives no choice between peace and war, only between fight or surrender. If we continue to accommodate, continue to back and retreat, eventually we have to face the final demand, the ultimatum..." - Ronald Rogan, A Time for Choosing Speech, October 27, 1964.

Here Reagan is saying that there is only so much one can accommodate. There is only so long one can be pacifist before ones enemies ask for a price greater than any other.

"He (Nikita Khrushchev) believes this because from our side he's heard poisonous pleading for peace at any price, or better red than dead, or as one commentator put it, he'd rather live on his knees than die on his feet. And therein lays the road to war, because those voices don't speak for the rest of us. You and I know and do not believe that life is so dear, and peace so sweet as to be purchased at the price of chains and slavery." - Ronald Rogan, A Time for Choosing Speech, October 27, 1964.

Here Reagan is giving the answer to what price he was talking about earlier. He claims that pacifism and accommodation will lead to the enslavement of a free people.

In summary, Pacifism renders people helpless in the face of adversity; pacifism also enables evil in the world. That is why total pacifism is morally indefensible. The largest flaw with pacifism is the fact that there are only so far you can go and only so much you can accommodate. Now bear in mind that Ronald Reagan was not a warmonger. Otherwise the Cold War would have been a lot bloodier. Ronald Reagan wanted peace with the Soviet Union, but he knew the road to peace was not Pacifism.

Non-Aggression Principle

According to Wikipedia, Non-Aggression principle is a concept in which aggression is inherently wrong. Therefore, under the framework of the Non-Aggression principle, rape, murder, deception, involuntary taxation, government regulation, and other behaviours that initiate aggression against otherwise peaceful individuals are considered violations of this principle. This principle is most commonly adhered to by libertarians. A common elevator pitch for this principle is, "Good ideas don't require force."

The general objection to the Non-Aggression Principle among philosophers is that it basically moves the goalposts one step back. Instead of trying to work out right and wrong, it says all wrong are things which cause aggression. The debate then becomes, what is aggressive? This is itself something incredibly difficult to answer. Does insulting someone break the non-aggression pact? Who and what are we entitled to be aggressive to in the first place? (Criminals, the mentally ill, attackers, in marriage, sexual relationships, and children as corporal punishment) What do we do if someone breaks the Non-Aggression Principle?

The idea that one cannot instigate force might be believed by a deontologist, but it would not be believed by a consequentialist, and it is not at all clear why we ought to believe one over the other due to the Non-Aggression

Principle. Discourse ethics like that of Jürgen Habermas gives a good argument for some variant of Non-Aggression Principle, but he goes well beyond what libertarians want from the principle. Non-Aggression Principle does not really have 'arguments' for its position, but rather is just coincidentally believed in some form by some other people who have non- Non-Aggression Principle -related arguments in its favour.

Non-Aggression Principle answers in many cases is not intuitive; it rather seems to be so out of line with common sense, that philosophers do not use them. There is a general principle in both Hobbes and Rawls, which is that you should test beliefs against your intuitions, and the more out-of-line your argument is with common sense, the more likely you have made a mistake somewhere on the way. Non-Aggression Principle typically concludes things like 'the government ought not to exist except as a voluntary night-watchman' (and even then, I think that's pushing the principle too far), and furthermore implies anything that, leads to third-party harm invalidates a contract (e.g. pollution, social degradation, etc.) These conclusions are so out of whack with most people's intuitions that it makes Non-Aggression Principle difficult to substantiate.

Satyagraha
Satyagraha is a philosophy and practice of nonviolent resistance developed by Mohandas Karamchand Gandhi. He deployed satyagraha techniques in campaigns for Indian independence and also during his earlier struggles in South Africa. The word satyagraha itself was coined through a public contest that Gandhi sponsored through the newspaper he published in South Africa, Indian Opinion. Etymologically, this Hindi word means 'truth-

firmness', and is commonly translated as 'steadfastness in the truth' or 'truth-force'.

Satyagraha theory influenced Martin Luther King Jr., James Bevel, and others during the campaigns they led during the civil rights movement in the United States. The theory of satyagraha sees means and ends as inseparable. Therefore, it is contradictory to try to use violence to obtain peace.

The problem of satyagraha is that truth itself, which it is a big proponent of, is not absolute.

There are no eternal facts, as there are no absolute truths. – Friedrich Nietzsche

Democratic peace theory

Democratic peace theory posits that democracies do not go to war with each other. The 'soft' version of the theory is that democracies are less likely to go to war with each other, and the 'hard' version is that democracies never go to war with each other, because of the accountability, institutions, values, and norms of democratic countries. In terms of norms and identities, it is hypothesized that democratic publics are more dovish in their interactions with other democracies, and that democratically elected leaders are more likely to resort to peaceful resolution in disputes. In terms of structural or institutional constraints, it is hypothesized that institutional checks and balances, accountability of leaders to the public, and larger winning coalitions make it harder for democratic leaders to go to war unless, there are clearly favourable ratio of benefits to costs. In either form it is a theory that has a relatively long pedigree (at least going back to Immanuel Kant), and ironically was part of the ideological reasoning for the United States invading Iraq (if Iraq and by example its neighbours could be turned into stable democracies, there would be no more conflict in the region).

I dislike the democratic peace theory is because it's basically un-falsifiable –we could provide a number of examples to disprove the theory, but there will always be counter-arguments as to why they do not 'count'. A big issue comes from defining the terms. What is a stable democracy? Can we consider the United Kingdom parliamentary system in the 19th century as democratic? What of the antebellum United States which denied disenfranchised significant portion of the population? What about the somewhat democratic system of Imperial Germany? How that is defined changes a lot of the results for war between democracies.

Democratic Peace Theory should first and foremost be understood as a theory of politics and international relations, and not a historical statement of fact. It principles do not actually claim that war between two liberal democracies is impossible –rather, it exists to qualify and explain a clear statistical outlier: The fact that liberal democracies do not seem to go to war against each other, and then seeks to explain why this may be so.

All the same, the fundamental thrust of the claim is true, despite the occasional lack of depth as to the reason behind it. The simple fact is, liberal democracies do not seem to go to war with each other very often, even when they are neighbours, and even when they might have some legitimate grievances.

However! The reason I mentioned above that democratic peace theory is a political theory and not a statement of historical fact is because there are, in fact several examples of wars between countries we would call liberal democracies, though crucially I think that these broadly serve to reinforce the political theory (the exception that proves the rule), despite denying democratic peace theory advocates the pure historical truth of the claim.

To look at the democratic peace theory claim that liberal democracies do not go to war against each other, we need to broadly ask what a liberal democracy is. I think it would be fair to say that we could anchor the time period looked at from 1750 on one end (a couple of decades before polities like the French Republic or the United States popped up, but a time in which already the United Kingdom and the Swiss Confederacy might reasonably be called democracies, and liberal for their time), all the way to 2000.

Looking at that time period the democratic peace theorists are vindicated in that vanishingly few of them are between liberal democracies. But not quite none! The Second World War made for some interesting circumstances, and provides us two decent examples that contravene democratic peace theory.

First, we have the British attack on the French fleet at Mers El-Kebir, as well as some other wider engagements in the Mediterranean in the wake of the Fall of France. The simplified version of the story is that, in the wake of the German capture of Paris and impending surrender of France, the Royal Navy attacked and destroyed the French fleet at Mers El Kebir to prevent it falling into German hands. As the Vichy government had not yet been formed by the time of the attack (48 hours away), the technical truth is that Britain attacked and destroyed an allied fleet belonging to the liberal French Republic. For obvious reasons, I think this does not present a cogent counter point to Democratic Peace Theory.

A slightly more difficult example is also from the Second World War. In the Winter War between Finland and the Soviet Union, Nazi Germany offered assistance to the Finns; during the war that followed afterwards, known as the Continuation War, Finland and Germany fought against the Soviet Union in Finland. However, due to the circumstances of the wider Second World War, the Soviet Union was aided in its war on Finland (and Germany) by the United Kingdom. This 'strange bedfellows' situation meant that the United Kingdom and Finland, both liberal democracies, were at war with each other, allied as they were to the Soviet Union and Germany, respectively. Again, I do not think this presents a very cogent counter to democratic peace theory, though it is at least a more significant conflict than a single attack as was Mers El Kebir.

There is one example of two liberal democracies at war, however, that I think does raise some curious questions about how universally applicable democratic peace theory is –The War of 1812. While also set against the backdrop of major international turmoil (the Napoleonic Wars), the war was essentially instigated by one liberal democracy (the United States) attacking a constituent part of another liberal democracy (Dominion Canada, and thereby the United Kingdom), due to mutual grievances over economics, some maritime laws being broken, some reasonably imperious British naval behaviour at sea, and historical grievances from the American War of Independence. The war was a significant manpower and military expenditure for both sides, and for the United States, the war was potentially existentially threatening, as the British Army famously captured and destroyed the United States capital of Washington DC. The war ended in a rather muted fashion with restoration of pre-war borders (with the exception of a few bits of land that went to Canada), and I think it is fair to attribute this relative restraint at least in part to shared cultures, shared views of liberalism, and shared economic interests. But the point still stands that two major, Western, liberal democracies fought a major war against each other with significant destruction and loss of life; it is the best counter example against democratic peace theory that I am aware of.

Democratic peace proponents will sometimes try to refute this example by claiming that one side or the other does not fulfil the requirements of being a liberal democracy, most often by claiming that Canada was not a liberal democracy as it was part of the British Empire; which is hogwash, in my opinion, because Canada had at that time a representative legislature as the United States had, and it could certainly be argued that Canada was more liberal on many issues than the United States, as the United States at the time struggled mightily with issues on immigration, slavery and representation. Even beyond that, there is no defence in focusing on Canada's status, as it was the United Kingdom proper that sent troops to invade the continental United States and capture cities like Washington, Baltimore and New York.

I can bring up another scenario I have found, digging around in datasets. This one you will need to bear with me on, because it is very specific, namely the 'Second Peace Operation' phase of the Turkish invasion of Cyprus on August 14-16, 1974. The democratic government of Archbishop Makarios was overthrown by a military coup on July 15, 1974, supported by the then military junta in Greece (hoping to unify the island with Greece). This triggered the first Turkish invasion on July 20, which ultimately led to the collapse of the coup plotters, the collapse of the Greek military junta, the restoration of

Makarios, and the opening of Cypriot-Turkish negotiations on July 25. Those negotiations broke down, and in August Turkey resumed its offensive, occupying 37% of the island of Cyprus. This was a direct military conflict between the nationally democratic Turkey and the restored nationally democratic Cyprus. It also should meet our casualty threshold.

Another scenario is the Cod Wars of 1958-1976 between the United Kingdom and Iceland, which meets our democracy test, because both nations were stable democracies at the time. These were conflicts over fishing zones that saw the Icelandic Coast Guard attempt to force out the British fishing ships protected by the Royal Navy out of the claimed Icelandic exclusive fishing zone. The ships of these two fleets did ram each other, but casualties were minimal. Is that the result of both countries being liberal democracies? Or being in NATO and not wanting to upset the United States too much?

All the same, I think the War of 1812 is an excellent example of the exception that proves the rule, because it is such an outlier. I also do not think it renders democratic peace theory obsolete at all; rather, I think it should inform us that democratic peace theory clearly has serious weight of evidence behind it, and is very valid, but is not the ultimate be-all end-all of geopolitics.

Balance of power

The principle of Balance of power is not to create hegemon, because hegemony dominates other states, reducing their autonomy and independence. In balance of power politics, stronger states are likely to dominate others and attempt to become a hegemon. Conversely, weaker states will defend themselves and prevent others from becoming a hegemon through balancing. In it, states increase their own power against sources of threat or targeted states, either by strengthening their own power or creating an alliance with other states. The classical realist position is that the key to promoting order between states, and increasing the chances of peace, is the maintenance of a balance of power between states –a situation where no state is so dominant that it can 'lay down the law to the rest'.

Balance of power principle was a central tenet of classical liberalism, among English liberal thinkers of the late 19th and early 20th century that free trade promoted peace. During the economic globalization in the decades leading up to World War I, writers such as Norman Angell argued in 1913 that the growth of economic interdependence between the great powers made war between them futile and therefore unlikely.

Balance of power theory works hand in hand with balance of threat theory, which posits that the alliance of behaviour of states is determined by the threat that they perceive from other states. States generally balance threat by allying against a perceived threat to deter the aggressor state. A successful balance of power/ threat leads to deterrence.

PEACE THROUGH DETERRENCE

Deterrence Theory refers to the scholarship practice of how threats, or limited force by one party can convince another party to refrain from initiating some other course of action. Deterrence is a psychological concept, and also an omnipresent concept. The only requirement is that it considers the parties involved as rational actors, if a state were irrational, deterrence would not work.

The concept of deterrence became prominent during the Cold war era, with the end of nuclear monopoly previously enjoyed by USA. In the Cold war era, the bombing of Nagasaki and Hiroshima gave it a new form– nuclear deterrence. State actors knew that no amount of conventional deterrence would be enough to challenge United States hegemony, so both the United States and the Soviet Union's security policy during the Cold War period was based on nuclear deterrence. In this period, the only way to avoid war was to achieve the doctrine of mutually assured destruction (MAD); this meant developing a second-strike capability. Another way to look at deterrence is the way it can be achieved. Direct deterrence means building one's own nuclear capability, like the United States. Extended deterrence means being under the umbrella of an actor which pursues direct deterrence policy, like South Korea under the United States.

When applying deterrence to the nuclear dimension, the whole dynamics of deterrence becomes more stable at keeping nuclear exchange at bay.

Explaining the theory further, 'A' can deter 'B' by threatening to use nuclear weapons, if 'B' does not act in accordance to it. For successful implementation of deterrence, 'B' has to consider 'A's' threat as credible.

In case another country possesses nuclear weapons, let say 'C', the theory then holds that 'A' would be deterred from attacking 'C', resulting in a dead-lock. In addition to this, if 'C' protects 'B' under its umbrella, then 'A' would be deterred from attacking 'B' because of the fear of getting attacked by 'C'. Basically, if 'A' has a monopoly on nuclear weapons, then it can threaten other states without fearing a reprisal.

For Deterrence to work properly and effectively, some assumptions must be taken into account.

- The actors involved must be rationale.
- The risk must be excessively higher compared to possible gain.
- The theory usually holds in a bi-polar setup where two or more powers exist.
- The nuclear power clearly addresses to the adversary what is considered as an unfavourable act and does not pass ambiguous message.
- The adversary is convinced that the coercer has the capability and the resolution to inflict unacceptable damage.

The theory of deterrence works only when the above mentioned assumptions are accepted. Another way of analysing the theory of deterrence is through a solution concept in game theory called Nash equilibrium.

Nash Equilibrium

Nash Equilibrium is a concept of game theory where the optimum outcome of a game is one, where no player has an incentive to deviate from his/her chosen strategy after considering an opponent's choice. Overall an individual can receive no incremental benefit from changing actions assuming other players remains constant in their strategies. A game may have multiple Nash equilibriums or none at all.

To test for a Nash Equilibrium, one has to simply reveal each player's strategy to all players; the Nash Equilibrium will exist if no player has changed their strategy despite knowing the actions of their opponents. For example let examine a game between Tom and Sam, in this simple game both players can choose:

(a) Receive a Dollar or
(b) Lose one Dollar

Sam		Tom	
		Receive a dollar	Lose a dollar
	Receive a dollar	1,1 *	1,0
	Lose a dollar	0,1	0,0

Table 5.1- A Nash equilibrium table of Sam to Tom

Key: (x, y) = payoff to Sam, Payoff to Tom

1= best, 0= worst

* Nonmyopic equilibrium

Logically both players would choose strategy (a) and receive a pay of one dollar each. If you reveal Sam's strategy to Tom and vice versa you will realize that no player deviates from their original choice. Knowing the other player moves means little and does not change their strategy.

To further explain Nash Equilibrium, I will use the prisoner Dilemma scenario. Let say, Mr Blue and Mr Red have each been arrested for some minor crime. The police think they (Mr Blue and Mr Red) have committed a more serious crime but they (The police) do not have enough evidence to convict them, they need a confession. The police then take them to separate rooms so they cannot talk to each other, and play a little game.

To try to force a confession the police give them two choices:

- Either they (Mr Blue or Mr Red) admit that their partner committed the crime and go scot-free, they (Mr Blue or Mr Red) will be pardoned for their minor crime but their partner will have to spend 3 years in prison.
- Or if they (Mr Blue or Mr Red) stay silent and their partner confesses that they (Mr Blue or Mr Red) were the one who really did it then they (Mr Blue or Mr Red) will be sentenced to 3 years in prison.

They (Mr Blue and Mr Red) know that the police do not really have any evidence to support their claim, and if they both stay silent, they will only go to prison 1 year each, for their minor crime, but if they both betray each other, then they will go to jail for 2 years each.

		Mr Blue	
		Cooperate	Defect
Mr Red	Cooperate	1,1 *	3,0
	Defect	0,3	2,2

Table 5.2- A Nash equilibrium table of the Prisoners Dilemma

Key: (x, y) = payoff to Mr Red, Payoff to Mr Blue

         3= worst, 2= next worst, 1= best

         * Nonmyopic equilibrium

In this scenario, cooperation (staying silent) between the two will give a better outcome (1, 1), but since the suspects see that they will gain by betraying the other, they are likely going to betray (Defect) each other (2, 2).

From Mr Blues perspective, If he does not snitch, he is probably going to spend 3 years in jail, because Mr Red would likely snitch on him, and goes scot free. If perhaps Mr Red does not snitch and he snitches, he will be free and Mr Red would spend 3 years in jail, so Mr Blue goes with the rational option, he decides to snitch.

From Mr Reds perspective, If he does not snitch, he is probably going to spend 3 years in jail, because Mr Blue would likely snitch on him, and goes scot free. If perhaps Mr Blue does not snitch and he snitches, he will be free and Mr Blue would spend 3 years in jail, so Mr Red goes with the rational option, he decides to snitch.

According to the Nash Equilibrium, despite that each player is perceived to know the opponent strategies, they are unwilling to change their initial strategy since there is nothing to gain by changing their strategy, Hence, both players stick to their initial strategies rather than switching to a new strategy.

Nash Equilibrium in Deterrence

According to Wikipedia, Nash Equilibrium has been used to analyse hostile situations such as wars and arms races, and also conflict may be mitigated by repeated interaction. In international political Theory, the prisoner's dilemma is often used to demonstrate the coherence of Strategic realism, which hold that in international relations, all states regardless of their internal policies or professed ideology, will act in their rational self-interest given international anarchy.

A classic example is the Cold War. During the Cold War the opposing Alliances of NATO and the Warsaw Pact both had the choice to arm or disarm. From each sides point of view, disarming whilst their opponent continued to arm would have led to military inferiority and possibly and annihilation. Conversely arming whilst their opponent disarmed would have led to superiority. If both side chose to arm, neither could afford to attack each other, but both incurred the high cost of developing and maintaining a nuclear Arsenal. If both sides chose to disarm, war would have been avoided and there would be no costs.

		Soviet Union	
		Arm	Disarm
United States	Arm	Compromise, War of Attrition (2,2) *	United States Victory, Soviet capitulation (4,1)
	Disarm	Soviet Victory, United states capitulation (1,4)	Compromise (3,3)

Table 5.3- A Nash equilibrium table of the Cold War

Key: (x, y) = payoff to United States, Payoff to Soviet Union

4= best, 3= next best, 2= next worst, 1= worst

* Nonmyopic equilibrium

Although the best overall outcome was for both sides to disarm, the rational course for both sides was to arm, and this is indeed what happened. Both sides poured enormous resources into military research and armaments in a war of attrition for the next 30 years until the collapse of the Soviet Union in 1991. The same logic could be applied in the previous scenario where the best overall outcome for both individuals (Mr Blue and Mr Red) was to cooperate (staying silent) and spend a year in prison for their minor charges, the rational cause prevailed, they both betrayed each other and had to spend two years in prison each.

You can see that in the Cold, War both sides avoided nuclear disarmament to deter their opponents from using their military superiority to annihilate the other. This Nash equilibrium created by both sides resulted in Deterrence and ushered in the illusion of Peace we are experiencing now called Pax Atomica.

Iterated Prisoner's Dilemma

If two players play Prisoner's dilemma more than once in succession and they remember previous action of their opponent and change their strategy accordingly, the game is called an iterated prisoner's dilemma. The iterated version models transactions between two people requiring trust and cooperative behaviour.

Let me use the prisoner's dilemma scenario between Mr Blue and Mr Red to explain the iterated prisoner's dilemma. In this scenario Mr Blue and Mr Red will be given multiple plea bargain to either snitch or cooperate with each other, and each individual would be informed of the other individual choice after a round of plea bargain (A round here denotes one period of successive choices between Mr Blue and Mr Red). According to the rule of this game their choices adds to their prison sentences. Let take a three round plea bargains for example.

In the first plea bargain both individual snitch on each other and get a jail sentence of two years each, in the second round of the plea bargain, if Mr Blue snitches and Mr Red stays silent, Mr Blue would remain on his two years jail sentence while Mr Red will have three more years added to his jail term. In the third round of plea bargain, if the results of the second round were repeated, Mr Blue would remain on his two years jail sentence, while Mr Red will have three more years added to his jail term, giving him a successive total of eight years gathered from the three rounds of plea bargain. The aim of this game is to get a lower jail term than your opponent, so in this case Mr Blue wins.

	Mr Blue						Total years
Mr Red	Round 1		Round 2		Round 3		
	Co-op	Defect	Co-op	Defect	Co-op	Defect	
Co-op	0,0	0,0	0,0	3,0	0,0	3,0	8,2
Defect	0,0	2,2	0,0	0,0	0,0	0,0	

Table 5.4- A Nash equilibrium table of the Iterated prisoner dilemma

Key: (x, y) = payoff to Mr Red, Payoff to Mr Blue

3= worst, 2= next worst, 1= best

* Nonmyopic equilibrium

From this game what do you think would be the best strategy to get a lesser amount of years in jail than your opponent? Well this was actually done in a series of computer programs that were all placed apart and forced to compete over and over again. The three strategies that were used were the defector, tit-for-tat and co-operator. The defector will always rat their opponent out, the co-operator will never rat his opponent out, and a tit-for-tat would start out not ratting out and then mimic whatever his opponent last move was.

Defector vs. Defector

	Defector						Total years
	Round 1		Round 2		Round 3		
Defector		Co-op	Defect	Co-op	Defect	Co-op	Defect	
	Co-op	0,0	0,0	0,0	0,0	0,0	0,0	6,6
	Defect	0,0	2,2	0,0	2,2	0,0	2,2	

Table 5.5- A Nash equilibrium table of the Iterated prisoner dilemma

Key: (x, y) = payoff to Defector, Payoff to Defector

3= worst, 2= next worst, 1= best

In a three-round plea bargain between a defector and a defector strategist, they would both betray each other and get a total of 6 years each, with no clear winner. This strategy of defector against defector, proved to be the most dangerous, and irrational of all strategies, because in tally both individuals would spend a total of 12 years in prison. A defector vs. defector strategy is one where there is no show of deterrence, both individuals did not consider the strategy of the other and both 'went for the kill', they both chose their selfish interest which cost them both. If a defector vs. defector strategy was at play in international relations, a nuclear apocalypse would have happened. Results from this strategy, showed why deterrence is necessary for some sort of stability or peace.

Co-operator vs. Co-operator

	Co-operator						Total years
	Round 1		Round 2		Round 3		
Co-		Co-	Defect	Co-	Defect	Co-	Defect	

			op		op		op		
	Co-op	1,1	0,0	1,1	0,0	1,1	0,0		3,3
	Defect	0,0	0,0	0,0	0,0	0,0	0,0		

Table 5.6- A Nash equilibrium table of the Iterated prisoner dilemma

Key: (x, y) = payoff to Co-operator, Payoff to Co-operator

3= worst, 2= next worst, 1= best

In a three-round plea bargain between a co-operator and a co-operator strategist, they would never betray each other and get a total of 3 years each; it is a win for both parties. In a co-operator vs. co-operator strategy, both individuals consider the choices of the other individual and decide to work together for peace, which turned out to be less deadly because they both spent a total of 6 years in prison. Co-operator vs. Co-operator strategy is more likely practiced by friendly countries with mutual institutions, values, and norms.

Tit-For-Tat vs. Tit-For-tat

		Tit-for-tat						Total years
		Round 1		Round 2		Round 3		
Tit-for-tat		Co-op	Defect	Co-op	Defect	Co-op	Defect	
	Co-op	1,1	0,0	1,1	0,0	1,1	0,0	3,3
	Defect	0,0	0,0	0,0	0,0	0,0	0,0	

Table 5.6- A Nash equilibrium table of the Iterated prisoner dilemma

Key: (x, y) = payoff to Tit-for-tat, Payoff to Tit-for-tat

3= worst, 2= next worst, 1= best

A game between a tit-for-tat and a tit-for-tat strategist would simulate the result of co-operator versus co-operator; it is a win for both parties.

According to Wikipedia tit-for-tat is an English saying meaning 'equivalent retaliation'. It is also a highly effective strategy in game theory. An agent using this strategy will first corporate, then subsequently replicate and opponents previous action. If the opponent previously was cooperative, the agent is cooperative. If not, the agent is not. This is similar to reciprocal altruism in biology.

Tit-for-tat strategy was used in the First World War in a spontaneous non-violent behaviour called 'Live and Let Live' where troops dug in trenches only a few hundred feet from each other and would evolve an unspoken understanding where, if a sniper killed a soldier on one side, the other expected and equal retaliation, and Conversely, if no one was killed for the time, the other side would acknowledge this implied truce and act accordingly.

Another way tit-for-tat strategy has been used in international relations is called 'Buck passing'. Passing the buck in international relations Theory involves a tendency of nation states to refuse to confront a growing threat in the hopes that another state will. The most notable example was the refusal of the United Kingdom, United States, France and the Soviet Union to confront Nazi Germany effectively in the 1930s.

Defector vs. Co-operator

	Co-operator			Tot al yea rs
	Round 1	Round 2	Round 3	

	Co-op	Defect	Co-op	Defect	Co-op	Defect	
Co-op	0,0	0,0	0,0	0,0	0,0	0,0	0,9
Defect	0,3	0,0	0,3	0,0	0,3	0,0	

Table 5.7- A Nash equilibrium table of the Iterated prisoner dilemma

Key: (x, y) = payoff to Defector, Payoff to Co-operator

3= worst, 2= next worst, 1= best

In a three-round plea bargain between a defector and a co-operator strategist, the defector would win because the co-operator is choosing not to defect, causing the co-operator to accumulate a total of 9 years in jail to a defector 0 years. This strategy success is highly flawed because, no one would like to be taken advantage of or be the 'Nice guy' in a conflict. This strategy will only be plausible, if the defector is the stronger state and the co-operator is the weaker state. The stronger state would always trump the weaker state because they are no repercussions for their actions, and there is no deterrence.

For smaller states to avoid being trumped by bigger states, they need to breed deterrence between themselves and the aggressor. What better way to do this than using the balance of power theory.

The balance of power Theory in international relations as I have reiterated before suggests that States may secure their survival by preventing any one State from gaining enough military power to dominate all others. If one state becomes much stronger, the theory predicts that it will take advantage of its weaker neighbour, thereby driving them to unite in a defensive Coalition.

A defensive coalition with a stronger state can breed deterrence with the aggressor state leading to a Defector vs. Tit-For-Tat situation, as aggression is unprofitable when there is equilibrium of power between rival coalitions.

Defector vs. Tit-For-Tat

		Tit-for-tat						Total years
		Round 1		Round 2		Round 3		
Defector or		Co-op	Defect	Co-op	Defect	Co-op	Defect	
	Co-op	0,0	0,0	0,0	0,0	0,0	0,0	4,6
	Defect	0,3	0,0	0,0	2,2	0,0	2,2	

Table 5.8- A Nash equilibrium table of the Iterated prisoner dilemma

Key: (x, y) = payoff to Defector, Payoff to Tit-for-tat

3= worst, 2= next worst, 1= best

In a three-round plea bargain between a defector and a tit-for-tat strategist, the defector would win, but will incur more years in doing so because the tit-for-tat opponent will retaliate to the defector betrayal. A scenario like this between two nuclear powers in international relations would lead to mutual assured destruction (MAD).

Mutual assured destruction is related but distinct from deterrence according to philosophers, but I believe Mutual assured destruction is necessary for assured deterrence. Mutual assured destruction, as I have reiterated before is a doctrine of military strategy and national security policy in which a full-scale use of nuclear weapon by an attacker on a nuclear-armed defender with second-strike capabilities would cause the complete annihilation of both the attacker and the defender, because the defender would respond equivocally, similar to the tit-for-tat strategy.

Mutual assured destruction is based on the theory of rational deterrence, which holds that the threat of using strong weapons against the enemy prevents enemy's use of those same weapons. Deterrence relies on retaliatory strike or second strike capability.

Co-operator vs. Tit-For-Tat

	Tit-for-tat						Total years
	Round 1		Round 2		Round 3		
Co-operator		Co-op	Defect	Co-op	Defect	Co-op	Defect	
	Co-op	1,1	0,0	1,1	0,0	1,1	0,0	3,3
	Defect	0,0	0,0	0,0	0,0	0,0	0,0	

Table 5.9- A Nash equilibrium table of the Iterated prisoner dilemma

Key: (x, y) = payoff to Co-operator, Payoff to Tit-for-tat

         3= worst, 2= next worst, 1= best

A game between a co-operator and a tit-for-tat strategist would stimulate the result of co-operator versus co-operator; it is a win for both parties, because the tit-for-tat opponent would never defect until they are betrayed and the co-operator would never attack first. Absolute deterrence is at play here, and it is a win for both parties.

Given this behavioural diversity, which kinds of strategy are most successful? To answer this question, in 1980 Robert Axelrod conducted a famous experiment. He invited hundreds of scholars to enter an Iterated Prisoner's Dilemma tournament, submitting their agent's decision algorithm digitally. In a computer simulation, every agent played every other agent 200 times. Unlike mine where the strategy with the lowest cumulative utility was declared winner, in Axelrod game, the agent with highest cumulative utility was declared the winner.

Many agents employed quite complex strategies, using hundreds of lines of code. The surprising result was that simple strategies, including Tit-for-Tat, often proved to be superior. Axelrod described three properties shared among successful strategies:

Nice	Do not defect before it opponent does. In my experiment, nearly all of the lower-scoring strategies were nice (Tit-For-Tat and Co-operator)
Retaliating	Do not be a blind optimist. Retaliate is sometimes necessary In my experiment, non-retaliating strategies were viciously exploited by 'nasty' strategies (Co-operator)
Forgiving	Fall back to cooperating if the opponent does not continue to defect This stops long runs of revenge and counter-revenge, maximizing points (Tit-For-Tat)

While one-off Prisoner Dilemma games favour selfish behaviour, Iterated Prisoner Dilemma can favour strategies that feature reciprocal altruism, such as Tit-for-Tat. More generally, Iterated Prisoner Dilemma strategies do best if they are nice, retaliating, and forgiving. This in turn explains how certain facets of our social and moral intuitions evolved.

Reciprocal altruism
In Human psychology and sociology, Deterrence can be implied to prevent conflicts in relationships; one of such

methods is reciprocal altruism. Reciprocal altruism is when altruistic behaviours are performed because they increase the likelihood of repayment in the future. The theory of reciprocal altruism was first described by the evolutionary biologist, Robert Trivers. Reciprocal altruism is often discussed in the context of Game theory, particularly iterated prisoner's dilemma game. The prisoner's dilemma provides an elegant way to test cooperative behaviour in the simplified context of a game. If your partner corporate, you return the favour. If he or she cheats, you do the same.

Some scholars, point out that reciprocal altruism widely spread in international relations and human society, and international reciprocity is the foundation of the international community. States act in the confidence that their cooperative actions will be repaid in the long term instead of seeking for the immediate benefit, so reciprocal altruism can be seen as generally accepted standards in international relations. On a personal scale, some scholars believe that reciprocal altruism derives from the subjective feeling of individuals to compliance with social norms. Social norms can be argued to reduce individual level variation and competition, thus shifting selection to the group level, so human behaviour should be consistent with social norms.

The theory of evolution has shown us that biological systems are the product of an optimization process known as natural selection. Only genes that improve reproductive success win over evolutionary time. From this context, it has long seemed unclear how human beings (and other animals) came to express altruistic behaviour. One specific example of this is in the case of robins, which emit high-pitched warning calls in the presence of danger. A bird that provides a warning call is temporarily more apparent to predators, thus reducing its immediate fitness probability. However, the same bird may benefit in the future from warning calls from other birds. In a single encounter, it may provide the greatest benefit to an individual bird if it remains silent but over time, over many encounters, it actually benefits the bird most to alert the others as long as everyone follows this behaviour. Each player has the incentive to defect, but overall they will do better if they cooperate, or act altruistically. This application of evolutionary game theory leads to the rise of cooperation and altruism in animal societies.

In everyday life, individuals evaluate the outcomes of the other's moral decision and make corresponding behavioural responses, such as acting kindly to the other's helpful behaviour (Positive Reciprocity) and unkindly to the other's harmful behaviour (Negative Reciprocity). This kind of reciprocal behaviours happens not only when interactions involve the individuals directly (Direct Reciprocity), but also when these acts have been directed not to us, but to others (Indirect Reciprocity). Both positive and negative Reciprocity are vital for human cooperation, adaption, and survival.

The ultimatum game

Imagine you win $1 million in the lottery, but there is a catch. This is a new experimental lottery in which the state says you must share your winnings with a stranger. You get to decide how the money is split, but the other person can reject your offer. If the other person rejects it, you both get nothing. You get only one chance, and the two of you will never see each other again. How much do you offer? This is called an ultimatum game.

The ultimatum game is a widely used behavioural task in the research of negative reciprocity. In a typical ultimatum game, participants act as a responder and decide whether to accept a fair or unfair division of money suggested by a proposer. If the division is accepted, the money would be split as proposed; but if the division is rejected, neither one would receive anything. Participants commonly accepted offers when the divisions comply with the fairness norm (fair offers). Although participants could have obtained a certain amount of money by accepting the unfair offers, they rejected more offers (i.e., receiving nothing) as the extent of the proposer's norm violation increase (i.e., the offers become less fair), indicating the negative reciprocity and negative cost enforcement.

In a scenario where participants were to act as a proposer, they resulted in making high proposals to the responder. A possible explanation for why participants tend to make such high offers in the ultimatum game is less to do with reciprocal altruism than it is to avoid being punished. That is, the proposers are aware that the responders will react negatively to any offer that they perceive as unfair, thus leaving the proposers with nothing. In short, proposers, familiar with negative reciprocity, offer an amount that they believe will not fall victim to that aspect of human nature, and thus maximise – or perhaps satisfice – in relation to their final expected reward.

Negative reciprocity breeds deterrence, due to individuals being aware of the punishments that might suffice if they do not act fairly. Negative reciprocity can work properly and effectively, if the adversary is convinced that the other person has the capability and resolution to inflict unacceptable damage if treated unfairly.

So for one to be able to breed deterrence through negative reciprocity between individuals or between states at large, one must be capable of inflicting harm. In human relations, a person must be assertive, decisive, or in Friedrich Nietzsche term, the person must be an Übermensch.

DER ÜBERMENSCH

"The Übermensch shall be the meaning of the earth!
I entreat you my brethren, remain true to the earth, and do not believe
those who speak to you of supra-terrestrial hopes! ...
Behold, I teach you the Übermensch: he is this lightning, he is this
madness! ...
Behold, I am a prophet of the lightning and a heavy drop from the cloud:
but this lightning is called Übermensch" – Also sprach Zarathustra,
Prologue

In 1883, Friedrich Nietzsche published a book titled 'Also sprach Zarathustra', in which he elaborated his ethical ideal, the Übermensch. As a teenager Nietzsche had already applied the word Übermensch to Manfred, the lonely Faustian figure in Byron's poem of the same name who wanders in the Alps, tortured by some unspoken guilt. Having challenged all authoritative powers, he dies defying the religious path to redemption. Nietzsche's affinity with Manfred culminated in him composing a piano duet called Manfred Meditation, which he sent to his musical hero, Hans von Bülow. The maestro's bad verdict on Nietzsche duet put a decisive end to Nietzsche's career as a music composer.

For Nietzsche, the idea of Übermensch was more like a vision than a theory. From his concept, the Übermensch was a person, or for us, a character, who is able to be their own determiner of value; who rejects the norms of society and lives by his own moral code.

One might ask, how does the journey to becoming Übermensch begin? Well, the journey to becoming Übermensch begins by realizing that peace is the creation of man, (that cannot be achieved), and that the concept of *"world peace"* is no longer useful for answering questions about breeding harmony among individuals and states at large. To become an Übermensch, one must process certain characteristics, which include:

76

Self-Determination

By self-determination, Nietzsche talks about breaking away from the mainstream traditions and thoughts of their society— for the purpose of this book, the mainstream tradition exemplified here is "world peace." Nietzsche preaches that an Übermensch does not just follow the majority view of their community, state, or religion. They explore many of the possible perspectives, and question any and all outlooks. In order to achieve this, one necessarily must question, and assess the dominant viewpoints of their society (world peace). Even the basic structure and accepted morality of their society is open to question.

Nietzsche's self-determining person is autonomous, freethinking, and fiercely independent. At times, and possibly quite often, he will be a non-conformist and iconoclast. In fact, Nietzsche himself was the epitome of the iconoclast: one who attacks or ignores cherished beliefs and long-held traditions due to the beliefs being based on error, superstition, or a lack of creativity.

In some sense the blind following of others and the failure to questions society's ideas and values make us less than human—for it is the human capacity to question and to be truly unique which makes life both interesting and fulfilling, or so Nietzsche believed. One should be 'sovereign' over their beliefs, free from the common and often counterproductive ideas and values of others, and stand apart from or beyond conventional morality, what Nietzsche calls 'supra-moral'. He expresses this when he describes the sovereign individual as *"liberated again from morality of custom, autonomous and supra-moral."* Additionally, the idea of achieving World Peace can be seen a conviction, and Nietzsche's Übermensch has no hardened convictions since convictions likewise stifle one's self-growth.

Creativity

Because Nietzsche's nihilistic views left humans in the position of having no single or overarching purpose that applied to all people, he believed that each of us would have to create the meaning and purpose for our own life. The creation of meaning and purpose, the creation of our character through our own authentic views and morals, the creation of our personality and style, and the joy of artistic and other creations was a constant theme for Nietzsche. Nietzsche declares that the *"noble type of man ... is value-creating."*

It is the human ability to create which sets him apart from other beings, and the more creative one is, the more they deserve to be admired. The Übermensch sees the world every day with new eyes, and gives the world and its events new interpretations. It is man who creates the ideas that a sunset is beautiful or that a spider is ugly. Nietzsche recognizes as such when he declares: *"Man believes that the world itself is filled with beauty—he forgets that it is he who has created it. He alone has bestowed beauty upon the world—alas! Only a very human, all too human beauty."*

Becoming

Nietzsche, similar to Socrates and Confucius, sets forth as one of the driving forces to a good life, is that of continual self-growth or as Nietzsche puts it, a life of becoming instead of just being. This involves pushing one's limits and going further than one has gone in the past. Nietzsche declares in Thus Spoke Zarathustra: *"With you I broke whatever my heart revered; I overthrew all boundary stones and images."*

78

The connection between self-determination and becoming is evident since questioning one's society will result in one changing themselves. However, people are often afraid to do so, and become comfortable in living a rather monotonous life with virtually the same ideas, values, opinions, judgments, goals, and actions as they had when they were relatively young. **They have ceased becoming, they just exist.** They have lost the joy of self-growth, the joy of letting go of one's past to create a new future and a new self, the joy of becoming by self-overcoming.

Of course, part of creation involves destruction, for it is from the destruction of our own viewpoints that we can start anew and create new ones.

Overcoming

Nietzsche believed that each of us needs challenges. While some religions and philosophies teach us to seek peaceful and contented lives, and to avoid competition, contention, hardship, heartache, and hindrances. Nietzsche believed that it is through overcoming challenges that the human spirit soars. That is how we become greater and better than we were before. Indeed, overcoming obstacles is needed for our self-growth, and the bigger the obstacle the more potential there is for personal growth. It is through our attitude and will, that we can overcome the challenges in our lives.

The importance of this attribute cannot be overstated as Nietzsche specifically described his own life in these terms: *"My humanity is a constant self-overcoming."* Furthermore, when Nietzsche introduces the Übermensch, the first attribute he associates with him is overcoming.

One important example of overcoming presented by Nietzsche is the *"sovereign individuals"* who keep their promises even if they have to overcome seemingly impossible obstacles to do so. They will overcome circumstances, other people, and even fate itself in order to keep their word.

These acts of overcoming will make a person more resilient, more formidable, more dependable, and more accomplished. They are no longer subject to the will of others or of bad luck; rather, through challenges they become masters of their environment and of themselves. They no longer live with excuses, for it is the challenges which make them who they are. They overcome not only the outside world, but themselves in the sense that they must overcome their own fears, self-doubts, and prior limitations. We can see here, the connection between becoming and overcoming, as one's becoming is a self-overcoming.

Discontent

In Taoism the goal is to blend with nature, your surroundings, your situations, and the people you encounter; in Buddhism the goal is to obtain inner peace through the extinction of desires; and in Christianity at least one goal is to be thankful and contented for all God has provided you. Nietzsche's recommendation is a radical departure from these age-old wisdoms. He tells us to never be contented and to continually strive for more, to embrace and pursue many of our desires, to triumph over the situations and people who would stand in the way of our life-affirming goals, and to welcome chaos and discontent within ourselves—for it is this discontent which spurs us on to do the unusual, to achieve the exceptional, to make great discoveries, and to literally create a new world. Nietzsche makes this point in his typically jarring way when he declares, "*Alas, the time of the most despicable man is coming, he that is no longer able to despise himself."*

Dissimilar to the age-old and supposedly wise classical teachings, Nietzsche believed that contentment is not a worthy goal for a human being. Rather, seek to make your mark, to grow as a person, to achieve what was once thought to be unachievable, to create what does not yet exist, and to change yourself and the world so that it moves in a new direction, with a new purpose, and to a 'higher' place. As Nietzsche wrote, *"What is great in man is that he is a bridge and not an end."*

Flexibility

Nietzsche believes that one should not live by inflexible rules handed down by society. Rather, as an autonomous and self-determining being, one should create their own ideas, standards, and goals by which to live and guide their lives. These guidelines would be provisional so they could change and evolve over time—as the person and the situations change.

Nietzsche's biggest concern is the inflexibility he sees in Western morality and religion. According to Nietzsche, Christianity has imposed rules and restrictions that do not serve life and which the Church itself does not follow, and has exhibited an inflexibility that stifles individual creativity and freedom—in part by trying to inflict guilt and shame on those who refuse to follow, or fail to live up to Church teachings and rules. Nietzsche believed that many Christians self-righteously cling to their faith and convictions and thereby lose the flexibility that life demands. Nietzsche concludes: *"The words 'conviction', 'faith', the pride of martyrdom—these is the least favourable states for the advancement of truth."* The same can be applied to the zeitgeist of peace in the 21st century, handed down to the populace by oligarchs, in previous chapters I criticised the world institutions, living in double standards in regards to world peace.

Additionally, since people and cultures differ so dramatically, Nietzsche believed it is counterproductive that moral standards should be the same for all people. Just as there are many different kinds of people and societies, so there should also be many different acceptable moralities. In the same regards the same standards of peace cannot be applied to everybody, creating an institutionalized government to enforce world peace is futile.

Moreover, the accepted moral systems impose human judgments onto reality, but those judgments themselves are not facts. It is people who impose their views of morality onto those actions. For example, it may be a fact that you lied, but it is not a fact that your lying is moral or immoral. This would be a judgment. As such, Nietzsche claims: *"There are no moral facts whatever. Moral judgment has this in common with religious judgment that it believes in realities which do not exist."*

Inflexibility is not limited to morality and religion. In fact, philosophers and intellectuals are also often guilty of coming up with systems which are both rigid and oversimplify the world in a way which contradicts our own experiences. For example, the one-lined tests for determining right from wrong action as proposed by Mill's Utilitarianism and Kant's categorical imperative could not possibly be sufficient for the complex and myriad of situations which we face, and these inflexible tests often end up with immoral results. Kant tells us to avoid lying even when the intention is to save an innocent life, while Utilitarianism would sacrifice an innocent person for the amorphous greater good.

Self-Mastery

Although the Übermensch is a free spirit, in that he or she is unconstrained by conventional views, the Übermensch at the same time exercises self-discipline. This enables one to overcome obstacles, to create a new self and a new world, and to achieve one's goals. Freedom of thought is accompanied by disciplined thoughts, freedom of action is accompanied by disciplined actions, and the freedom to dream is accompanied by the discipline necessary to achieve those dreams.

Self-mastery will produce a life of achievement—a life of which one can be proud because one has demonstrated the self-discipline to overcome both idleness and excuses. The Übermensch takes responsibility for his or her life because their self-mastery allows them to overcome the hardships and challenges that deter and discourage others. They triumph in spite of life's many tests, and they often rise above the barriers or walls that others would find impenetrable.

Casual readers of Nietzsche are often taken by Nietzsche's concept of will to power, and sometimes mistakenly interpret his philosophy as essentially advocating the use of brute force or power against others. This, however, is to fail to understand what Nietzsche was trying to convey to us. The will to power's most important use is to aid us in mastering ourselves.

It is not a question of mastering others, of overcoming the herd by overpowering it. The herd to be overcome is the herd in us. Mastery and overcoming are to be understood as self-mastery and self-overcoming primarily. After one has learned to have mastery over them, then this mastery necessarily manifests itself in one's relations with others and the outside world.

Self-Confidence

One of the driving forces of Nietzsche's philosophy is his repudiation of the Christian emphases on guilt and sin—which cause people to feel ashamed of whom they are. They are made to feel they are not worthy of love or success. These ideas drain the self-confidence of an individual. One needs this self-confidence to not only achieve things, but also to feel happy and fulfilled.

The first three chapters of Nietzsche's book Ecce Homo are titled: "*Why I Am So Wise*", "*Why I Am So Clever*", and "*Why I Write Such Good Books.*" I do not think he wrote these chapters because he was an egomaniac, or narcissistic, or conceited, or arrogant. It seems that his purpose is to let the reader know that we are more productive when we feel good about ourselves and further, that it is beneficial for one to be proud of their victories, accomplishments, creations, and triumphs. As Nietzsche said, "*The noble soul has reverence for itself.*" Along these lines, it is counterproductive to be ashamed of thinking and acting as humans naturally think and act: we need not feel guilty for being lustful or revengeful (Negative Reciprocity) or angry, nor for wanting to lead or even dominate others. These are normal human instincts and attributes.

Indeed, without self-confidence it becomes almost impossible to achieve and therefore to be proud of yourself. Nietzsche's Übermensch feels good about him or herself, and believes that their life is turning out well and will continue to do so. They believe so because of their attitude about themselves, and because they have the confidence that they will overcome the challenges they face. The Übermensch exudes self-confidence. Nietzsche makes this clear when referring to those of a noble nature: *"In the first case, when the ruling group determines what is 'good', the exalted, proud states of the soul are experienced as conferring distinction. They are happy to stand out from the mainstream as they view themselves in not only a good light, but in a superior light.*

Cheerfulness

The Übermensch is characterized by a cheerful attitude toward life. By being cheerful, Nietzsche does not mean that one is always smiling; rather, he is recommending that we welcome life and its challenges with open arms—that we appreciate the experiences and opportunities which life offers. As he puts it, the Übermensch says *"yes"* to what comes their way, not deterred by society's rules and prohibitions which would keep one from fully living and appreciating life. Like a child, one should explore life with wonder and awe, not deterred by societal judgments.

The Übermensch appreciates both all that life has to offer and all aspects of themselves. They are able to maintain this cheerfulness in spite of the challenges and tragedies that enter their lives. Because they accept life as it is, they can appreciate the hardships as much as the joys. Both contribute to their personality and resilience. Both help make them the person who they are.

While Christianity, with its notion of heaven, and Hinduism and Buddhism, with their notion of achieving nirvana and thereby going into an existence where the self or individual is extinguished, focus on the other-worldly, Nietzsche taught us to keep our focus on this world and this life—as that is all we can be sure that we have. Be appreciative and cheerful here and now.

As an atheist, Nietzsche felt that even a life with much suffering was preferable to a life of eternal nonexistence, and therefore the most productive attitude was to appreciate everything. The pain you feel means you can still feel; the hardships you endure means there is a you to endure and overcome them; and the tragedies that confront the living means that they are still alive to rise above and transcend those tragedies. Nietzsche stated: *"Pain is not considered an objection to life: 'If you have no more happiness to give me, well then! You still have suffering.* To approach this gift of life in other than a positive manner is to not understand the gifts of consciousness, of feeling, of love, and of the bodily sensations. The Übermensch opens his eyes and his heart to all of creation—even in its harmful or evil manifestations—and finds a way to maintain a cheerfulness which welcomes and appreciates each day.

Moreover, because the Übermensch does not feel restricted by society's ideas, morals, beliefs, opinions, and rules, they are able to say "yes" to things which are forbidden to others. They are free to explore, to learn, to encounter, and to experience things that others feel constrained or forbidden to pursue. They can say "yes" to all of existence, and take delight in discoveries which were not open to those who follow the herd. This, too, brings cheerfulness into one's life.

Courage
The Übermensch is not reluctant to be a leader, to face challenges, to dominate situations and people, or to effectuate change. This takes courage and strength and is exhibited through the exercise of one's will to power.

All successful people and leaders know how to wield their will to power. They conquer, achieve, overcome, dominate, and emerge victorious by the fearless exercise of their strength, by the powerful exercise of their will. They dare to dream when others have abandoned hope, they dare to push forward when others have surrendered, they dare to overcome when others have capitulated, and they dare to succeed when others have failed. They explore new ideas—often upsetting the majority when they do so. They put their ideas, their dreams, and sometimes their lives in jeopardy.

I think it is easy to misread Nietzsche and misunderstand his focus. He is primarily concerned with spiritual or internal courage, not with the mundane virtue of courage in physical battle. Nietzsche is recommending we create and manifest the spiritual courage to pursue what we believe is important even when, and perhaps especially when, our beliefs go against those in the majority. Courage is not mainly about the physical conquering of others; rather, it is about the courage to think and do what you consider to be valuable even when forbidden or restricted by those in power—sometimes knowing that there will be personal consequences. It is the courage to be a truly self-determining individual who is not reluctant to go against the dominant views of one's society, the courage to become and thereby to transform oneself, and the courage to overcome obstacles no matter how daunting they may seem or be.

Think how courageous Nietzsche had to have been to have taken on Christianity and European morality. Think what courage it took for him to label himself an "immoralist" (because he dared to question conventional morality, not because he did immoral acts). Consider what it would have been like for Nietzsche to announce that he was an atheist and that the Christian conception of God was not believable. We can recognize the overwhelming scorn and criticism he must have faced. In these respects, Nietzsche displayed a spiritual courage rarely seen in the world.

We can think of courageous people such as this: Gandhi, Abraham Lincoln, and Martin Luther King, Jr. They did not shy away from the formidable challenges they faced. They displayed their courage with enormous demonstrations of their will to power, and thus were able to change the world. In some sense, they imposed their will on the rest of the world. They set the agenda. They shaped and determined their society's values. As the words at the start of every Star Trek episode declared, they dared to *"boldly go where no man has gone before."*

ACKNOWLEDGMENT

As much as i would love to take all the credit for this book, they are a lot of people who had a hand in making his dream come to life. I am particularly grateful to Enoabasi Ekwere Davies, who proofread this book with diligence and care. I also want to thank my readers, who have stuck through this whole epic roller coaster of a saga, and diligently read this book to the end. I'm also grateful to everyone who jogged my memory and who contributed to my amazing life. Thank You.

REFERENCES

THE CONCEPT OF PEACE IN INTERNATIONAL RELATIONS

"Allied Democratic Forces Insurgency - Wikipedia.", 1 Feb. 2022, https://en.wikipedia.org/wiki/Allied_Democratic_Forces_ insurgency.

"Cabinda War - Wikipedia." 1 Feb. 2019, https://en.wikipedia.org/wiki/Cabinda_War.

"Casualties of the Syrian Civil War - Wikipedia.", 1 Apr. 2020, https://en.wikipedia.org/wiki/Casualties_of_the_Syrian_ci vil_war.

"Colombian Conflict - Wikipedia.", 26 Feb. 2006, https://en.wikipedia.org/wiki/Colombian_conflict.

"Insurgency in Cabo Delgado - Wikipedia.", 1 May 2018, https://en.wikipedia.org/wiki/Insurgency_in_Cabo_Delga do.

"Insurgency in the Maghreb (2002–Present) - Wikipedia." *Insurgency in the Maghreb (2002–Present) - Wikipedia*, en.wikipedia.org, 26 Oct. 2014, https://en.wikipedia.org/wiki/Insurgency_in_the_Maghreb _%282002%E2%80%93present%29.

"Internal Conflict in Myanmar - Wikipedia.", 2 Apr. 1948, https://en.wikipedia.org/wiki/Internal_conflict_in_Myanm ar.

"Iraqi Conflict (2003–Present) - Wikipedia.", 1 Oct. 2020, https://en.wikipedia.org/wiki/Iraqi_conflict_(2003%E2%80%93present).

"Kivu Conflict - Wikipedia.", 15 Mar. 2015, https://en.wikipedia.org/wiki/Kivu_conflict.

"Kurdish–Turkish Conflict (1978–Present) - Wikipedia.", 16 Feb. 2021, https://en.wikipedia.org/wiki/Kurdish%E2%80%93Turkish_conflict_(1978%E2%80%93present).

"Lord's Resistance Army Insurgency - Wikipedia.", 1 Nov. 2021, https://en.wikipedia.org/wiki/Lord%27s_Resistance_Army_insurgency.

"Mali War - Wikipedia." *Mali War - Wikipedia*, en.wikipedia.org, 1 Apr. 2022, https://en.wikipedia.org/wiki/Mali_War.

"Mexican Drug War - Wikipedia.", 11 Dec. 2006, https://en.wikipedia.org/wiki/Mexican_drug_war#:~:text=When%20the%20Mexican%20military%20began,demand%20along%20with%20U.S.%20functionaries.

"Moro Conflict - Wikipedia." *Moro Conflict - Wikipedia*, en.wikipedia.org, 1 Feb. 2021, https://en.wikipedia.org/wiki/Moro_conflict.

"Nagorno-Karabakh Conflict - Wikipedia.", 11 Oct. 2020, https://en.wikipedia.org/wiki/Nagorno-Karabakh_conflict.

"Nigerian Bandit Conflict - Wikipedia.", 25 July 2021, https://en.wikipedia.org/wiki/Nigerian_bandit_conflict.

"Papua Conflict - Wikipedia.", 1 Aug. 2019, https://en.wikipedia.org/wiki/Papua_conflict.

"Philippine Drug War - Wikipedia.", 6 Mar. 2019,
https://en.wikipedia.org/wiki/Philippine_drug_war.

"Rojava–Islamist Conflict - Wikipedia.", 1 Nov. 2019,
https://en.wikipedia.org/wiki/Rojava%E2%80%93Islamis
t_conflict.

"Russo-Ukrainian War - Wikipedia.", 3 Feb. 2022,
https://en.wikipedia.org/wiki/Russo-ukrainian_war.

"Somali Civil War - Wikipedia." g, 1 June 2020,
https://en.wikipedia.org/wiki/Somali_Civil_War.

"South Sudanese Civil War - Wikipedia.", 1 Jan. 2021,
https://en.wikipedia.org/wiki/South_Sudanese_Civil_War.

"Sudanese Conflict in South Kordofan and Blue Nile -
Wikipedia, en.wikipedia.org, 5 June 2011,
https://en.wikipedia.org/wiki/Sudanese_conflict_in_South
_Kordofan_and_Blue_Nile.

"Tigray War - Wikipedia.", 1 Feb. 2022,
https://en.wikipedia.org/wiki/Tigray_War#:~:text=All%2
0sides%2C%20particularly%20the%20ENDF,of%20hum
anitarian%20aid%20into%20Tigray.

"War in Darfur - Wikipedia.", 1 Sept. 2016,
https://en.wikipedia.org/wiki/War_in_Darfur.

"War on Terror - Wikipedia.", 1 Apr. 2018,
https://en.wikipedia.org/wiki/War_on_Terror.

"Yemeni Civil War (2014–Present) - Wikipedia.", 29
May 2018,
https://en.wikipedia.org/wiki/Yemeni_Civil_War_(2014%
E2%80%93present)#:~:text=The%20Yemeni%20Civil%2

0War%20(Arabic,with%20their%20supporters%20and%2
0allies.

Clauset, Aaron, Trends and fluctuations in the severity of
interstate wars AU, Science Advances, 4, 2, (2022)
https://doi.org/10.1126/sciadv.aao3580

THE CONCEPT OF PEACE WITHIN PEER GROUPS

"Friendship Is Just a Symbiotic Relationship - Bishwas
Bhandari." *Bishwas Bhandari*, bishwas.net, 22 Feb. 2022,
https://bishwas.net/friendship-is-just-a-symbiotic-
relationship.

INTRAPERSONAL PEACE

Kahneman, Daniel, 1934- author. Thinking, Fast and
Slow. New York :Farrar, Straus and Giroux, 2011.

Ribáry G, Lajtai L, Demetrovics Z, Maraz A.
Multiplicity: An Explorative Interview Study on Personal
Experiences of People with Multiple Selves. Front
Psychol. 2017 Jun 13;8:938. doi:
10.3389/fpsyg.2017.00938. PMID: 28659840; PMCID:
PMC5468408.

THE ZEITGEIST OF PEACE

"Balance of Threat - Wikipedia.", en.wikipedia.org, 1
Aug. 2019,
https://en.wikipedia.org/wiki/Balance_of_threat#:~:text=
According%20to%20the%20balance%20of,threat%20to%
20protect%20their%20own.

"Democratic Peace Theory - Wikipedia." *Democratic Peace Theory - Wikipedia*, en.wikipedia.org, 1 June 2020, https://en.wikipedia.org/wiki/Democratic_peace_theory.

"Peace - Wikipedia.", 10 Dec. 2020, https://en.wikipedia.org/wiki/Peace.

"Peace And Order In The Development Of The Country Research And Process Essay Example - PHDessay.Com." *Free Essays - PhDessay.Com*, phdessay.com, 3 Oct. 2016, https://phdessay.com/importance-of-peace-and-order-law-in-the-development-of-the-country/.

"R/AskHistorians - In My Political Science Module, We Learned the Democratic Peace Theory, Which Says No Mature Liber Democracy Has Ever Gone to War with Another. Is This True?" *Reddit*, www.reddit.com, https://www.reddit.com/r/AskHistorians/comments/ojesfk/in_my_political_science_module_we_learned_the. Accessed 4 Aug. 2022.

"The Decline and Fall of the United Nations: Why the U.N. Has Failed and How It Can Be Reformed | The Heritage Foundation." *The Heritage Foundation*, www.heritage.org, https://www.heritage.org/report/the-decline-and-fall-the-united-nations-why-the-un-has-failed-and-how-it-can-be-reformed#. Accessed 4 Aug. 2022.

PEACE THROUGH DETERRENCE

"Re-Examining the Nuclear Deterrence Theory." *Aditi Malhotra*, aditimalhotra.com, 2 Nov. 2010, https://aditimalhotra.com/2010/11/02/re-examining-the-nuclear-deterrence-theory-2/.

"Oliver, Adam. "A Dash of Behavioural Economics (Chapter 4) - Reciprocity and the Art of Behavioural Public Policy." *Cambridge Core*, www.cambridge.org, 1 July 2019,
https://www.cambridge.org/core/books/abs/reciprocity-and-the-art-of-behavioural-public-policy/dash-of-behavioural-economics/4F2EAAFCD80D111CF156A68C5F26AA18.

Experimental Economics and Experimental Game Theory Daniel Houser, Kevin McCabe, in Neuroeconomics (Second Edition), 2014
"Prisoner's Dilemma - Wikipedia.", 1 Nov. 2012,
https://en.wikipedia.org/wiki/Prisoner%27s_dilemma.

"Buck Passing - Wikipedia.", 6 June 2017,
https://en.wikipedia.org/wiki/Buck_passing.

"Reciprocal Altruism in Humans - Wikipedia.", 1 May 2021,
https://en.wikipedia.org/wiki/Reciprocal_altruism_in_humans.

DER ÜBERMENSCH

"Nietzsche’s ÜBermensch: A Hero of Our Time? | Issue 93 | Philosophy Now." *Nietzsche’s ÜBermensch: A Hero of Our Time? | Issue 93 | Philosophy Now*, philosophynow.org,
https://philosophynow.org/issues/93/Nietzsches_Ubermensch_A_Hero_of_Our_Time. Accessed 4 Aug. 2022.

Publishing, Scientific Research. "Nietzsche's Best Life: The Ten Greatest Attributes of the Ubermensch, & a Comparison to Aristotle's Virtuous Person." Nietzsche's Best Life: The Ten Greatest Attributes of the

Ubermensch, & a Comparison to Aristotle's Virtuous Person, www.scirp.org, 31 Aug. 2017, https://www.scirp.org/html/8-1650804_78855.htm.

INDEX

97

101

ABOUT THE AUTHOUR

FRANCIS JEREMIAH SHARON is an author, and freelance copywriter. He is currently a student, studying biochemistry (BSc) at Michael Okpara University of Agriculture, Umudike. His novel book *The Illusion of Peace in Social Hierarchy* has been featured on Amazon, Okadabooks, and all over the Web. He currently resides in Abia State, Nigeria.

For more information on the author, reach out to him via email at Francisj2nd@gmail.com.

COPYRIGHT

THE ILLUSION OF PEACE IN SOCIAL HIERARCHY. Copyright © 2022 by Francis Jeremiah Sharon. All rights reserved. No part of this text may be reproduced, transmitted, downloaded, decompiled, reverse-engineered, or stored in or introduced into any information storage and retrieval system, in any form or by any means, whether electronic or mechanical, now known or hereafter invented, without the express written permission of the Author.

FIRST EDITION

Cover and interior illustrations and cover design by Canvas.

Print ISBN: 978-1-38-779057-9

www.ingramcontent.com/pod-product-compliance
Lightning Source LLC
Chambersburg PA
CBHW070816050426
42452CB00011B/2065